Rethinking Wetland Archaeology

DUCKWORTH DEBATES IN ARCHAEOLOGY

Rethinking Wetland Archaeology

Robert Van de Noort
&
Aidan O'Sullivan

Duckworth

First published in 2006 by
Gerald Duckworth & Co. Ltd.
90-93 Cowcross Street, London EC1M 6BF
Tel: 020 7490 7300
Fax: 020 7490 0080
inquiries@duckworth-publishers.co.uk
www.ducknet.co.uk

A catalogue record for this book is available
from the British Library

ISBN 0 7156 3438 0
EAN 9780715634387

Typeset by Ray Davies
Printed and bound in Great Britain by
CPI Bath

Contents

List of Figures

Prologue and Acknowledgements

Both of us were born in wet countries; in the Netherlands (where the water rises from below) and the Republic of Ireland (where it falls from above). Moving around England, Wales and Northern Ireland, we have both also been lucky to have spent much of our archaeological careers working in wetland archaeology. Each of us has spent summers in different places, digging prehistoric wooden trackways on raised bogs, struggling through estuarine saltmarshes and mudflats, or splashing around at the edge of crannogs. So we both have memories of many times spent with larks singing above us, breezes ruffling the surface of the water around us, and of that literally sinking feeling as the water inevitably seeped into our boots. Wetland archaeology remains a constant theme in our lives, despite all the other tasks we have set ourselves.

However, in recent years, we have both felt that wetland archaeology is a discipline that has perhaps reached an impasse of sorts. This small book has been many years in the making and reflects this unease. Our first discussions date back to 1998, during the 'Recent advances in wetland archaeology' conference at University College Dublin, where we realised that we shared similar concerns about the direction wetland archaeology had taken (and had not taken). One of the reasons for the long gestation of the book was that we wished to find the right balance between taking a critical view of wetland archaeology, showing an appropriate respect towards the work of long-serving practitioners in the field, and our desire to stir up this area of work and cause a paradigmatic shift in the archae-ological study of wetland landscapes. We hope that the result of this searching is seen as a genuine attempt to rejuvenate wetland archaeology; and, whilst maintaining the best aspects of the tradition of wetland research that now goes back some four decades, as an attempt to reintegrate it with mainstream archaeological debate and thus allow wetland archaeology to contribute fully to our understanding of the past.

We acknowledge the patience and encouragement of Deborah Blake of Duckworth and the series editor, Professor Richard Hodges. Our work as wetland archaeologists has been enlivened by many collaborations and conversations over the years, and we acknowledge the inspiration of Martin Bell, John Bradley, Joanna Brück, Richard Brunning, Gabriel Cooney, Melanie Giles, Jon Henderson, Leendert Louwe Kooijmans, Conor McDermott, Cara Murray, Cathy Moore, Nigel Nayling, Robert Sands, Michael Stanley, Stephen Rippon and Wijnand van der Sanden. This book has been read (in parts) in draft stage by Barry Raftery, John and Bryony Coles, Gabriel Cooney, Robert Sands, Tim Lankshear and Graeme Warren, and we are grate-ful for the comments we have received and frequently incorporated into the text. Simon Denison checked our English and ensured readability.

Finally, our gratitude goes to Professor John Coles, pioneer and advocate of wetland archaeology *extraordinaire*, to whom we dedicate this book. We thank him for his enthusiasm and inspiration.

1

Why we need to rethink wetland archaeology

Introduction

Wetland archaeologists have been involved in recent years with some of the most spectacular archaeological discoveries around the world, typically revealing the diversity of past people's cultural, social and economic responses to wetland environments. Wetland archaeological surveys and excavations in estuaries, rivers, lakes and bogs have often uncovered settlements, trackways and even human bodies in sometimes remarkable states of preservation. Star Carr, Friesack, Windover, Tybrind Vig, the Alpine Lake settlements, Alvastra, the Sweet Track, Flag Fen, 'Seahenge', the Dover Boat, the Corlea 1 trackway, Biskupin, Glastonbury Lake Village, House Q in the Assendelver Polder, Lagore and Ballinderry crannogs, the wooden masks from Key Marco, Ozette on the north-west coast of the USA, and the bog bodies from Tollund, Grauballe and Lindow – these are all sites and finds from wetlands. In coping with the unique and welcome challenges of waterlogged sites, wetland archaeologists have typically adopted multidisciplinary approaches (looking at pollen, seeds, insects, wood and microorganisms) to enable high quality reconstructions of past people's daily lives and practices. Wetland archaeologists working with the general public have also managed to communicate the real excitement of working on waterlogged archaeological sites.

As an identifiable specialist field within the broader discipline of archaeology, the origins of wetland archaeology can be found in the 1960s, although the first excavations in wetlands go back to the 1840s (see J. & B. Coles 1996). Wetland archaeology has certainly been an undoubted success since then, as shown by the numerous conferences, projects and reports that have been published under that label, especially in Europe, the Americas, Japan and Australasia. However, as has happened in other specialist fields within archaeology, for example maritime archaeology and environmental archaeology, wetland archaeology has become somewhat isolated within mainstream archaeology despite its many accomplishments, with the consequence that the results of our specialist research frequently do not reach those working outside the field (see McGrail 2003).

Moreover, it has to be said that the wetland archaeological programme has not been unproblematic. In its theoretical approaches, it could be argued that wetland archaeology retains a strong empirical, functionalist core. Some have suggested that wetland archaeologists are so impressed by the quality of their archaeological evidence that they imagine that they have only to uncover their sites to be able to simply 'read the past' from waterlogged structures, sediments and seeds without further theoretical analysis. Indeed, this has sometimes been presented as the defining feature of wetland archaeology. On the other hand, some have argued that wetland archaeologists' interpretation of people's activities in wetlands have tended towards environmental determinism, exploring only an exploitative relationship between people and their environment.

Interestingly, there seems to be relatively little conflict, debate or controversy about these issues within the wetland archaeological community (but see Evans 1992 and Gearey 2002 for the exceptions that prove the rule). Perhaps this is simply because international wetland archaeological conferences, organised under the auspices of the Wetlands Archaeological Research Project (WARP), have mainly been forums where exciting new discoveries are presented, or where problems of investigation are explored, but where sites can rarely be discussed in terms of their own cultural and social context. This often leads to a situation in which, for example, fishtraps or baskets from different parts of the world (e.g. America, Japan and Europe) are discussed, described and compared, while their social and cultural contexts are barely touched on. In a sense, this is a predictable result of what might be called 'wetlands internationalism' – that is, the coming together of wetland archaeologists from around the world at specialist conferences to compare their wetland discoveries. What connects the speakers is archaeological preservation and research techniques, rather than any particular expertise in comparing cultural or social groups separated in place and time.

The external view

Wetland archaeology has certainly been criticised from outside the field, especially at the time of the beginning of the post-processual 'movement' in the late 1980s and early 1990s. For example, it was criticised by Chris Scarre in 1989, Christopher Evans in 1990, Christopher Tilley in 1991 and Colin Haselgrove *et al.* in 2001. Chris Scarre (1989, 274) praised the quality of the individual papers in the edited volume *European Wetlands in Prehistory* (J. Coles & Lawson 1987), but warned that 'the volume indicates the potential danger that the very quantity and quality of the remains from waterlogged sites may obscure the important question as to where all these discoveries are leading us. Most of the chapters are basically descriptive, and one cannot help feeling that the true strength of wetland archaeology will be shown only when it is used to reassess the prehistoric development of entire regions.' He concludes that it

11

is unlikely that many non-specialist readers would be willing to purchase the book.

Christopher Evans' (1990) book review of *Wet Site Archaeology* (Purdy 1988) states that wetland archaeology seems to have been engaged in 'multi-period internationalism', in which different wetland sites around the world were simply to be linked together and compared because of their preservation, and explanation and interpretation tended towards functional universals and environmental determinism. Evans describes wetland archaeology as having become both globalised and isolated, in that wetland specialists from across the world meet up regularly to discuss their experiences, and pursue their studies primarily with relevance to each other rather than to the 'dryland' archaeologists who work in the areas adjacent to the wetlands. Evans (1990, 340) claimed that wetland archaeology should instead be about 'the dynamic interactions of environments and societies, the muck of life'.

Christopher Tilley (1991), reviewing *People of the Wetlands* (B. & J. Coles 1989), also wrote that while wetland archaeology can provide us with startling arrays of empirical evidence, from Iron Age bodies to Neolithic chewing gum, in the interpretation of this evidence it provides little sense of the people who created this evidence as social beings. 'People of the wetlands', he complained, seem to be regarded as simply 'bodies requiring tools, shelter, clothing and full stomachs of fish and fowl', but that was all. In his opinion, there was little attempt to explore how the 'people of the wetlands' constructed distinctive social worlds through material forms.

Such a critical external view of the separateness of wetland archaeology still persists. For example, the recently published research framework for the British Iron Age is unequivocal about this (Haselgrove *et al.* 2001, 11), and calls for the 'need to overcome the conceptual separation which still characterises many wetland projects, where the emphasis is on the wetland to the exclusion of the wider landscape with which it was articulated'.

Admittedly, many of these reviews were written some years ago, and they were aimed to some extent at books that may have been largely populist or internationalist in their objective. It could also be claimed that in reality, most scholars working in wetland projects have been well aware of theoretical developments and have used those aspects of theory that seem to work for them. This is particularly true of those projects (whether on estuaries, lakes or bogs) that are essentially landscape archaeology projects that happen to be set in a wetland environment, such as the Humber wetlands and the Severn estuary in Britain, or of recent studies of Neolithic and Bronze Age lake settlement in southern Germany.

Why we need to rethink wetlands

Nevertheless, the necessity to rethink wetland archaeology – that is, to engage with the broader theoretical discussions in archaeology, to set wetlands research in broader geographical contexts and to become more relevant to 'mainstream' archaeology – is still alive today. From the selected reviews quoted above, it is evident that we are not the first who seek to critique wetland archaeology, either from within or outside the field. However, to date, no constructive suggestions have been put forward that show the way ahead.

This book aims, then, to help rethink the archaeological study of wetlands. It is written by two archaeologists who have spent the best part of their lives studying, surveying and excavating in wetlands, and it is intended to stimulate discussion and debate on how a new agenda for the archaeological study of wetlands for the coming years can be developed. It will do this by setting out examples from our own and others' work that are fully contextualised, or integrated with mainstream archae-

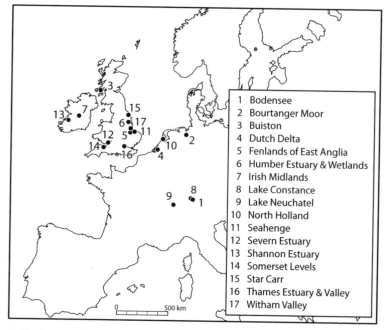

1 Bodensee
2 Bourtanger Moor
3 Buiston
4 Dutch Delta
5 Fenlands of East Anglia
6 Humber Estuary & Wetlands
7 Irish Midlands
8 Lake Constance
9 Lake Neuchatel
10 North Holland
11 Seahenge
12 Severn Estuary
13 Shannon Estuary
14 Somerset Levels
15 Star Carr
16 Thames Estuary & Valley
17 Witham Valley

1. The location of the major studies used in this book.

ological practice and theory, and which thus illustrate the gains of rethought wetlands. This need for geographical contextualisation – that is, the recognition that wetlands should be studied within broader regional frameworks – has now been widely recognised (e.g. J. Coles 2001; and in 2000 the British Academy organised the two-day conference 'Contextualising Wetlands'), but the contextualisation we seek goes beyond this. This is best illustrated by a few examples.

One of the world's pre-eminent wetland sites is the Neolithic Sweet Track, in the Somerset Levels in south-west England (B. & J. Coles 1986). The track, and the research that revealed it, are in all aspects remarkable. Its initial construction date is exact. Dendrochronological dating has placed it in 3807/6 BC, and it is Britain's oldest known road. Its 'biography' is known in great detail. The design of the track is unambiguous, and tree-species analysis has shown us the range of tree species used, which types of tree were used for each component of the track, and also how the timber had been transformed from timber to planks and stakes. The track had been built from wood from a mature primary, secondary and deliberately managed woodland with primary woodland producing the majority of oak planks and secondary and managed woodland the straight rods and poles of ash, hazel and oak. Dendrochronological analysis has shown that repairs were carried out up to ten years after the initial construction date, with at least one oak plank felled three years, two ash planks seven years and several hazel pegs cut eight and nine years after the construction of the Sweet Track. The track was subsequently abandoned.

Palaeoenvironmental studies of samples taken from the peat matrix that surrounded the trackway have provided a clear understanding of the landscapes in which the track was built, and how this landscape changed over time, with the *Phragmites* and fenwood peats giving way to a raised moorland environment after the track had been abandoned. The excavators also found a range of tools and deposits alongside the track, including a jade axe and a ceramic pot containing a cache of hazelnuts. Nevertheless, despite its pre-eminence, the Sweet Track stands in splendid isolation, and remains a conundrum (B. Coles 1999). We do not know where the Sweet Track comes from, or where it goes to. We do not know who, or what, was linked as a result of its manufacture. It remains unclear what social, political, economic or religious objectives were achieved by it. In short, it is an un-contextualised site, and its full potential for understanding past behaviour has yet to be realised. Whilst there are ample reasons why the original research did not address this, as the research was undertaken against the background of large-scale peat extraction (see also below and Chapter 2), the lack of contextualisation remains.

Another good example of this problem is the study of prehistoric boats from intertidal contexts. No area has been more important to the study of prehistoric maritime structures than the North Ferriby foreshore in the Humber estuary in northeast England (Wright 1990). The finds from this area include the remains from at least three sewn-plank boats. These boats, named Ferriby, 1, 2 and 3 (or F1, F2 and F3), were built from hewn oak planks with bevelled edges, 'sewn' or stitched together by stitches of yew withies. An internal frame, comprising cleats integral to the planks and a system of transverse timbers, provided strength to the hull. The boats have been dated to the period around 1900 cal BC, the Early Bronze Age, and represent a significant innovation in the boat building technique of the time (Wright *et al.* 2001). This technique for boat building in the Early Bronze Age is unique to the UK, with other similar finds coming from Kilnsea in the outer Humber estuary, Dover, and from Caldicott in the Severn estuary (Van de Noort *et al.* 1999). Undated finds of cleats believed to represent boats have been found in the Tees and Solent estuaries. Considerable effort has been expended on the study of these boats. Following their excavation and publication, several sewn-plank boats have been wholly or partly reconstructed, and much has been learnt about the woodworking technology, woodland management, and the capacity and performance of these craft. However, the full potential of the study of these early boat remains in general, and those from North Ferriby in particular, have not yet been fully realised. We know practically nothing about the use of these boats, either in daily life, or as specialised long-distance craft. Few archaeologists have considered whether the North Ferriby site, by all accounts the only known prehistoric boatyard in western Europe, can be studied in a broader geographical context. Consequently, no serious attempts have been made to analyse the social and political aspects of boat building. The value of these maritime

studies on our understanding of the societies in Bronze Age
Europe thus remains minimal (see Harding 2000, 177-85).

The studies of the Somerset Levels and the North Ferriby
foreshore would both benefit from being placed within broader
frameworks (see English Heritage 1991). A broader geographical framework in the latter case would necessitate a
consideration of whether the sewn-plank boats are in any way
related to the funerary monuments constructed in the Early
Bronze Age on the Yorkshire Wolds, some 40 km to the north of
North Ferriby. Certain gravegoods from these monuments, such
as amber beads and Armorico-type bronze daggers, originate
from as far away as Continental Europe, and it seems likely
that the sewn-plank boats would have played a role in the
long-distance exchange that evidently existed. The role played
by the new type of boats in the socio-political and economical
changes that took place in the Early Bronze Age could then be
considered, and further insights could be gained into the role of
travel and long-distance exchange (Van de Noort 2004).

However, contextualisation of these wetland-based discoveries should not be limited to a geographical contextualisation
alone. New ideas, concepts and theories should also become
ingrained in the study of wetlands. Returning to the example of
the Sweet Track, merely expanding the study area may not be
the most fruitful approach, especially if Neolithic settlements
are archaeologically invisible, or never existed in the area.
Rather, a reconsideration of the primary function of the Sweet
Track as a transport route could be more productive. Should we
therefore, perhaps, approach the Sweet Track as a ritual monument, as an environment-specific reinterpretation of the
concept of a cursus or a causewayed enclosure? This would
provide a new framework for explaining the jade axe and pot
filled with hazelnuts, and the other probably votive deposits
such as the child's axe found alongside the track. Or should we
try to understand the symbolic significance of the track, across

a wild, uncultivated landscape, possibly as an attempt to draw the natural wilderness into the controlled, cultivated realm (Tilley 1994, 206-7)? Once the reed marsh had been crossed and symbolically conquered, it may have had no longer any practical use, and this may explain the short life-span of the Sweet Track. And how are we to interpret the repairs of the track some ten years after its initial construction? In the next chapter, we seek to reinterpret the Sweet Track within such frameworks.

While the incorporation of 'dryland' archaeology and its theoretical innovations would be of great benefit to wetland archaeology, the contribution of wetland studies to broader archaeological debates is equally undoubted. If wetland archaeology can overcome the drawbacks of remaining in isolation, in terms of archaeological theory, that contribution will be greatly amplified. Two further examples will illustrate this.

Many scholars of material culture have employed theoretical analyses to draw conclusions about gender, agency and symbolism. By default, the basis for such analyses lies with the material culture, but where organic remains are not preserved, this basis is highly biased. In their study of Palaeolithic Central and Eastern Europe, Olga Soffer *et al.* (2001, 233) argue that inorganic objects made up as little as 5% of prehistoric material culture, and therefore that such objects should not form a basis for 100% of explanations. This clarifies, in their view, the concealment in prehistoric studies of 'women, children and older individuals ... because technologies used [by them] are usually far more perishable than those [used] by males – an observation amply confirmed by cross-cultural ethnographic data on the division of labor by sex and the concomitant implements associated with the different tasks'. Only research that can include the organic material culture can therefore provide a genuine attempt to study this kind of subject matter. Such arguments, however, are rarely found in recent publications on material culture.

1. Why we need to rethink wetland archaeology

Similarly, archaeologists are accustomed to explaining the past in broad phases, each often lasting several centuries. This is a direct result of the dating tools they have available, principally typology and radiocarbon dating. Thus, the main phases of construction and occupation of a Neolithic or Bronze Age settlement, or Iron Age hillfort such as Danebury in southern England, are typically 150 to 200 years long (e.g. Cunliffe 1995). One must question whether such a chronology is adequate for explaining the actions, decisions and activities of the communities and individuals that lie behind the observations that form the archaeological record, issues of particular relevance if we want to understand agency in Iron Age society. We must also query whether such broad phasing can show the real-time dynamics of daily life. If a site like Danebury, or other similar hillforts in Europe with a long timespan but poor dating framework, had been occupied for a number of occasions for short periods, for whatever social or political reasons, would we have the tools to identify this?

Wetland studies have the potential benefit of dendrochronology and thereby opportunities to date structures and features much more accurately. The example of the Sweet Track has already been mentioned, but a more influential study is that of the lake dwellings on the German side of the Bodensee. It had been thought that a large number of lake-dwellings existed simultaneously here in the Neolithic period. Detailed analysis of the sequence of these sites on the basis of dendrochronology showed that the four lake settlements (of which one was occupied twice), one known dryland site and possibly three other settlements were established in sequence. Each of these settlements would only have been in use for 10 to 15 years, but no two of these sites ever co-existed (B. Coles 1999). More recently, dendrochronological analyses of the phasing of occupation on an early medieval crannog at Buiston, Scotland, revealed a startlingly, and perhaps alarmingly (for normative models of

19

long-lived medieval settlement patterns) dynamic picture of site occupation and abandonment (Crone 2000; Crone *et al.* 2001). Such studies of course cannot be replicated in environments where archaeological wood is not preserved, but the lessons that come forward from this type of wetland archaeology must be disseminated widely for their far-reaching consequences for prehistoric studies.

In short, these examples illustrate without doubt that contextualising wetland archaeology brings mutual benefits, both for those archaeologists who prefer their feet wet and for those who would rather keep them dry. By the nature of the evidence it studies, wetland archaeology can provide insights into aspects of the past that simply are not replicated in other contexts or environments. However, such contributions must be placed within current theoretical frameworks to be relevant for the wider archaeological community.

It would be quite incorrect to leave the impression at this point that such integration has not taken place at all. We find ample evidence of the geographical contextualisation of wetland studies. Leendert Louwe Kooijmans' study of 'wetland exploitation and upland relations of prehistoric communities in the Netherlands' (1993) is an explicit attempt to integrate the studies of the wetlands in the Dutch Delta and the 'uplands' further to the east. The main purpose of this paper was to redress the assumption of many Dutch archaeologists that wetlands were unpleasant environments for prehistoric people, and therefore that the study of wetlands was not representative of the wider context. On a very different scale, the work led by Francis Pryor (2001) on Flag Fen and the Fengate area of the East Anglian Fenlands incorporated both the wetland proper and an extensive part of the wetland margins. The results of this work have been extensively published and anyone who has taken note of it will agree that our appreciation of the prehistoric activities in this area has been much improved by the study of the varied landscapes. Without the wetland margins, the Flag Fen causeways and platform would not have been placed in the context of the long-term landuse and field systems that existed at Fengate and, conversely, the importance of the wetlands as seasonal pasture to the farmers who lived on the drier parts of the land could not have been fully appreciated if the wetland context had itself not been studied.

Many other examples could be presented here to contest the accusations made of an isolated wetland archaeology or 'wetlandism'. But despite this progress towards the placing of wetlands study in broader geographical contexts in the last few decades, the calls for a fully relevant wetland archaeology have not abated (e.g. Haselgrove *et al.* 2001). Why this continuing problem? We need to go back to the early days of wetland archaeology to find the answer.

The background to the current state of wetland archaeology

A very short history of wetland archaeology

The archaeological study of wetlands commenced with the excavations of the Swiss and other Alpine 'lake dwellings' from the 1850s onwards (Keller 1866), stimulating similar research elsewhere (e.g. Monroe 1882 in Scotland; Wood-Martin 1886 in Ireland; Cushing 1897 on the coast of Florida; and Bulleid and Gray 1911 in south-west England). An early form of wetland archaeology was established, although the term 'wetland' was never used (see Chapter 2 on the use of the term wetland), and the focus was principally on lake settlements.

Wetland research received a further boost in the first half of the twentieth century. Above all others, the research by Grahame Clark in the 1930s in the East Anglian Fenlands, where he closely collaborated with the palynologist Harry Godwin, and again in the late 1940s at Star Carr, were to define the direction of future archaeological research in wetlands. Grahame Clark had been strongly influenced by archaeological and palaeo-environmental work in Scandinavia, which had shown him the richness and possibilities of research in water-logged conditions that enabled functional, and environmentally contextualised, analyses. The excavations at Star Carr were initially published in 1954 and again in 1972 as '... a case study in bioarchaeology'. The excavations in this late-glacial lake in the Vale of Pickering in Yorkshire have become a type-site, not just for the information they produced for such early communities in post-Ice Age Europe, but also for the close integration of archaeological and (palaeo-) biological information, such as pollen, animal bones and archaeological wood. No other wetland site has received the same attention as Star Carr, and new ideas, concepts, methods and techniques that can be applied to the waterlogged remains of wetlands have all been applied or tested at this site and the surrounding landscape (e.g. Legge & Rowley-Conwy 1988; Mellars & Dark 1998; Conneller & Schadla-Hall 2003).

Elsewhere, we note parallel developments. For example, the Biologisch-Archeologisch Instituut (BAI) of the University of Groningen in the Netherlands was founded in 1920, unambiguously to progress the integrated study of archaeology and palaeo-biological aspects of the past. Unsurprisingly then, much of the research undertaken from the BAI focussed on wetlands, including the raised mires of Drenthe and the coastal wetlands adjacent to the Waddenzee.

The Somerset Levels Project heralds another phase in wetland archaeology. Commenced in 1963, it became a model for research into the, by then, again frequently ignored but extensively threatened wetlands of Europe and further afield. The success of the Somerset Levels Project has already been alluded to in the case of the Sweet Track (B. & J. Coles 1986). Many other trackways and platforms were found during the

1. Why we need to rethink wetland archaeology

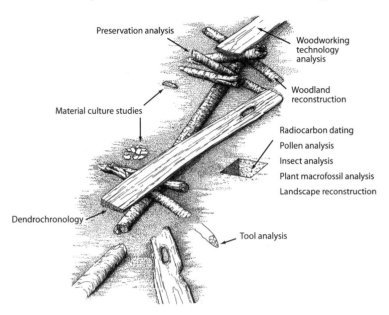

Preservation analysis

Woodworking technology analysis

Woodland reconstruction

Material culture studies

Radiocarbon dating
Pollen analysis
Insect analysis
Plant macrofossil analysis
Landscape reconstruction

Dendrochronology

Tool analysis

2. The richness of wetland archaeology, providing the source for multi-disciplinary studies made possible by the survival of organic remains (after Bryony Coles 1995: 2).

lifetime of the project. Co-operation with the peat-extractors, who caused widespread damage to the wetlands and the archaeological sites contained within them, played an important role in the discovery of many sites, including the Sweet Track. As was the case with Star Carr, a close integration of environmental and archaeological studies provided a level of detailed understanding that can only be achieved in wetlands. A case in point is the integration of archaeology and the analysis of plant and insect macrofossils that was pioneered by the project, alongside the effective use of high-resolution dating using dendrochronology.

The person in charge of the Somerset Levels Project was John Coles, joined in 1973 by Bryony Coles. John Coles had been taught by Grahame Clark, who introduced him to the

Somerset Levels. It is unsurprising that a degree of similarity existed between Coles' approach to archaeology, in both fieldwork and theory, and that of Clark. In his *History of Archaeological Thought*, Bruce Trigger (1990), describes Grahame Clark, alongside V. Gordon Childe, as one of the principal proponents of archaeological functionalism. This developed during the second quarter of the twentieth century, partly beside and partly replacing the cultural-historical paradigm. Many of the characteristics of the functional school of thought can be identified in the work in the Somerset Levels and other projects that developed in its shadow.

The functionalist archaeologists were, and continue to be, characterised by a positivist approach to science and the search for 'common sense' answers to the question posed by the archaeological record. This approach, considering what is functional and what is not, became, in the 1940s and 50s, increasingly an economic functionalism. This habitually translates to ecological or environmental determinism, that is, it becomes an approach in which environmental conditions and changes are seen as the chief reasons for the way in which people conduct themselves. Of course, archaeologists active in wetlands such as Grahame Clark and John Coles were not the only functionalist archaeologists, and even today, the basic principles of functionalism ('common sense') form the basis of much archaeological writing, especially where the archaeologists do not express an explicit theoretical stance. However, as wetland archaeologists had extensive access to palaeo-environmental sources, and were among the pioneers who integrated cultural and environmental research, the functionalism adopted by them tended to lean particularly heavily on the reconstruction of environmental change as the basis for understanding cultural change. Even where interpretations include considerations of ritual behaviour, this is often set in the context of environmental conditions, with religion becoming an extension of economic functionalism.

24

1. Why we need to rethink wetland archaeology

Similarly, the functionalist approach (often repackaged within processual or New Archaeology, which became the foremost theory-explicit form of archaeology in the 1960s) was and remains the key driver of wetland research in North America.

Leendert Louwe Kooijmans' (1993) paper, integrating the exploitation of the Dutch lowland wetlands and upland 'dry-lands', is a good example of this approach. As already stated, the main aim of this paper was to redress the widespread feeling that wetlands were perceived as 'unpleasant' land-scapes. It had been assumed that people had been driven to settle in the lowlands because of population pressure on the uplands. Louwe Kooijmans describes the main aim of this paper as 'a plea for an opposite approach: to conceive wetland settle-ment as a deliberate choice by prehistoric communities for the exploitation ... of these ecozones; not to consider the wetlands as being unsafe, but as offering attractive ecological conditions and a high natural productivity or agricultural potential' (p. 71). Interestingly, and not atypically for Dutch archaeology of that period, both the dryland and wetland archaeology pre-sented here approach the past within an environmentally deterministic paradigm. It would be disingenuous to suggest that wetland archaeology has not developed further than to look for the most plausible environmental explanation, but the preference for environmental change as the principle agent of cultural change remains strong (e.g. Casparie 1987; Brinkkemper 1991).

Another characteristic of functionalist archaeology is the rejection of the importance of generic theories and models, and a preference for more site-specific explanations. Within the processual or New Archaeology that developed in the late 1950s and through the 60s and 70s, the value of explicit theories and models is exemplified in David Clarke's *Models in Archaeology* (1972). John Coles (in Coles & Minnett 1995, 181-90) recently reappraised David Clarke's generic concept of Iron Age society in *Models*, providing a superb example of this diverging approach between functionalist and New Archaeology. Clarke's model was based principally on excavated evidence from the Glastonbury Lake settlement conducted in the period 1885-1907 by Arthur Bulleid and Harold St George Gray (1911). Clarke's reinterpretation depicts, amongst others, a model Iron Age household, comprising a major and minor house, and various huts, other outbuildings and platforms. This model has formed a basic building stone in our understanding of Iron Age society. John Coles' reappraisal respectfully, but resolutely and definitively, demolishes Clarke's model on the basis of a detailed reassessment of Bulleid and St George Gray's archaeological and more recent palaeoenvironmental evidence. Significantly, no new model is offered nor sought. This dislike of theory building, and an unwillingness to engage with theoretical archaeology, is shared with many other colleagues who gather the primary data through excavation and survey, both wet and dry.

Wetland archaeology and nature conservation

Although not necessarily connected to the functionalist approach, much of the archaeological work in wetlands from the 1960s, and especially in the 1980s and 1990s, has been linked to specific and extensive threats to the wetlands, and much research was essentially undertaken as rescue archaeology. The work in the Somerset Levels was linked directly to peat extraction, but projects around the world have been associated with the transformation of wetlands. Threats to wetlands include peat extraction (e.g. the Irish Midlands), drainage (e.g. Florida's Everglades), water abstraction and river diversions (e.g. the marshlands of Iraq), the conversion of land to arable landuse (e.g. the East Anglian Fens and the Dutch lowlands), urban and industrial developments affecting many river valleys, and global coastal erosion. This rescue aspect of wetland research has contributed significantly to the pressure on fieldwork and, consequently, to a disparaging feeling towards colleagues who are perceived as spending too much time thinking about, rather than saving, our wetlands.

In this context, wetland archaeology does not stand alone. The first meeting of the UNESCO-sponsored International Convention on Wetlands in 1971 in Ramsar, Iran, represented a sea-change in the world's attitude towards wetlands. The Ramsar Convention initially focussed on the protection and conservation of wetlands as habitats supporting migratory birds, but has since developed to become a vehicle for promoting wetlands world-wide for their broader biological and cultural values. Consequently, close co-operation between archaeologists and nature conservationists, in Britain and elsewhere, has been achieved to a degree that is rarely replicated in other areas, but it has also reinforced the emphasis on environment-culture interaction, rather than integration with 'mainstream' archaeology (e.g. Cox *et al.* 1995; B. Coles & Olivier 2001).

Returning to the development of wetland archaeology, it seems reasonable to suggest that the excellent preservation of the material culture of wetland sites, the abundance of source material for palaeoenvironmental reconstruction, and the extensive threats towards this friable resource have resulted in something of an embarrassment of riches of data, which has inhibited the engagement of wetland archaeology with mainstream theoretical debate. After all, archaeological theories are often developed to fill the bigger voids in our knowledge and understanding of the past. But this has contributed to the isolation of wetland archaeology. Despite the rise of New Archaeology and the post-processual critique of it, functionalist-based wetland archaeology has proved to be particularly resilient to theoretical advances. The role that individuals have played in this process cannot be ignored. The support given by many governmental agencies to wetland projects, within and outside the framework of the Ramsar Convention, has further contributed to a focus on the conservation of wetlands, management of the archaeological resource, and research that concentrated on the recording of the threatened heritage (e.g. *English Heritage Strategy for Wetlands*; Olivier & Van de Noort 2002). Whilst no one can deny the continuing need for such support, this focus has again contributed further to a minimal engagement with wider theoretical issues.

Rethinking wetland archaeology: developing the agenda

The aim of this book is to make wetland archaeology more relevant to, and interactive with, wider archaeological debates, or to stimulate the debate that will lead to this. It is not advocating a rejection of past values and achievements, but rather encourages a rejuvenation of the aims and purposes of wetland archaeology. If this can be achieved, then the importance of this friable and threatened component of our historic environment will only be further enhanced. We would also urge our colleagues from other fields to take another look at recent wetland archaeological projects, as we are confident that there are results that warrant consideration.

The organisation of this book

In each of the next three chapters, we will develop approaches to wetlands and wetland archaeology that fit within contemporary interpretative agendas in archaeology. These agendas are, to a large extent, derived from and developed in cultural geography and cultural anthropology, and resonate within a wider post-modern approach to the study of people and their environments.

Chapter 2 considers wetlands and landscapes. We will argue

that we need to accept that too often wetlands have been viewed within an exploitative economic framework. Wetlands are seen as places where people could fish, farm and gather raw materials and we see people's actions there as embodying rational, economic decisions. Obviously, these are very modern, even capitalist views of the world. Indeed, even the term 'exploit' is an ideologically loaded concept, rendering the landscape as an object out there to be used, transformed and managed. Perhaps we need to begin to start thinking about the ways that people inhabited, understood and imagined landscape as constitutive of the societies that they lived in (e.g. Lopez's 1986 'native eye'). On the other hand, we should not adopt an overly romantic view of wetlands as solely idealistic landscapes. People's ideas and beliefs about landscapes would have been shaped by the ways that they used and moved around them every day.

Chapter 3 approaches the 'people of the wetlands' (and we will look at this phrase again) as knowledgeable social agents. Previously, perhaps, there was a tendency in wetland archaeology to think that with our archaeological discoveries of footprints in the mud, bog bodies' stomach contents and toolmarks on pieces of worked wood, we could get closer to the individual. But this was often a peculiar de-socialised individual, the same the world over and across time. We need to think about people as living within particular historical societies, and that they lived, worked and moved through wetlands as the men and women of these particular societies. So we need to start thinking of people in wetland archaeology in terms of social identity. These were people who certainly lived in a world where they were constrained by social rules (or environmental processes), but they themselves created and altered that world by their actions and thoughts. We could also start exploring how wetland landscapes would have been contested by different social groups, along ethnic, class or gender lines. Finally and most importantly, we recognise that we are often looking at landscapes from the 'bottom up' and that particularly in wetland archaeology we are often looking at the everyday routines of ordinary people, and that this is the key to reconstructing social identities.

Chapter 4 considers the material culture from wetlands. High-resolution dating (e.g. through dendrochronology) has offered unsurpassed insights into the dynamic nature of past people's interaction with their material culture. However, the focus of recent research in cultural anthropology and archaeology on the biographies and life-cycles of objects and sites that are metaphorically linked to the lives of the people offers new ways of understanding material culture from wetland sites and landscapes. Dwellings and objects have cultural biographies linked to the changing cultural meanings given to them, and to changing perceptions of them. We will reconsider the evidence of the occupation and abandonment of an Alpine Neolithic lake village, the Iron Age houses at Goldcliffe, as well as the early medieval crannog at Buiston, and reinterpret these sites in terms of birth, life and death, and why places are abandoned and forgotten.

In Chapter 5 we will think about the ways in which wetland archaeologists interpret the past in the present. Wetland archaeologists are probably closer than other archaeologists to environmental sciences, with all the connotations of scientific practice and beliefs that that can bring. In truth, we are always interpreting our data through a 'cloud of theory', as Matthew Johnson (1999) has pointed out. It is striking, for example, that in recent years, intertidal archaeological surveys around Britain and Ireland have tended to find the same types of sites, i.e. Neolithic short-stay campsites, Bronze Age and Iron Age marshland huts and trackways associated with saltmarsh grazing or exploitation, or medieval fisheries. To what extent are projects finding what they would expect to find, informed as they are by each other's publications? We also need to think about wetland archaeology in terms of its political resonance. It might be claimed that wetland archaeologists, because of the frequent threat to their evidence, have tended to side with environmental protection. In modern Europe, most environmental protection schemes will be imposed top-down by regulation and government bodies. We have to be aware that in some cases, for example on an estuary or river, our concerns will not always match a local community's use of the landscape. On the other hand, we are also often linked with companies (such as Bord na Móna in Irish Midlands bogs) who sponsor wetland survey and excavation in raised bogs, and who have also long provided employment for the local community.

Finally, Chapter 6 offers conclusions, and considers whether there is a future for wetland archaeology.

*

The topics presented here are not exhaustive and other avenues of rethinking wetland archaeology could have been explored, for example a consideration of gender in wetland archaeology. However, within the context of this series, we believe that we provide ample basis for the debate as to how we might rethink wetland archaeology.

2

Places in watery worlds: thinking about wetland landscapes

Introduction

Over the last two decades, archaeologists have changed the way past landscapes have been studied. The literature on landscape is far too extensive to be even summarised here, but in essence this new way of looking at the landscape includes a major shift from a functionalist to a quite diverse range of social, ideological and symbolic approaches to understanding past landscapes. Landscapes have been studied by anthropologists in various ways, with particularly useful perspectives provided on the role of place-names in landscapes (e.g. Hirsch & O'Hanlon 1995; Basso 1996). Landscapes have been approached by historians exploring the ideologies behind landscape art and representation (e.g. Cosgrove and Daniels 1988), they have been approached as a metaphor and source of inspiration for literature and nation building (e.g. Schama 1996) and as a socially and politically contested space in the modern world (Bender 1993, 1998; Bender & Winer 2000). 'Landscape archaeologists' have explored landscape in terms of both 'natural' and 'monumental' landscapes, sometimes simultaneously (e.g. Bradley 2000), in terms of prehistoric ancestral geographies and kinship connections (Edmonds 1999) and, influentially, in terms of people's phenomenological experience and understanding of the worlds they move through (e.g. Tilley 1994; 2004).

Paraphrasing the words of the cultural geographer Dennis

2. Places in watery worlds

Cosgrove, we recognise that landscape is an ideological concept that is – or was – intended to represent the ways in which people in the past signified themselves and their world through their imagined relationship with nature (Cosgrove 1994, 15). In other words, past people should be understood as active rather than passive agents within the landscape, and the 'landscape' comprises more than archaeological sites and finds set against an environmental backdrop. We must also start to consider the broader range of elements (or phenomena) that were present in the past landscapes in the eyes of the people we study, such as time, space, daily activities, myths and stories, past and contemporary settlements, burial grounds and monuments and, of course, 'nature', which was not perceived as static but dynamic, and thus had agency. Among the most prominent published examples of this new approach we could mention Barrett (1994), Barrett *et al.* (1991), Bradley (1993; 1998; 2000), Bradley *et al.* (1994), Cooney (2000), Hill (1995), McOmish *et al.* (2002), and Tilley (1994), and edited volumes by Bender (1993) and Brück (2000).

This chapter considers a number of ways of thinking about wetlands in the landscape, adopting the principles employed in recent non-wetland landscape studies. However, one of the most important aspects of our argument is the need to understand the diversity of wetlands, and how people engaged with this diversity. Wetlands encompass an extraordinarily wide range of physical landscapes, including raised bogs, fens, lacustrine and riverine wetlands and coastal and estuarine saltmarshes, and we need to deconstruct the 'meta-narrative' of wetlands, and start seeing these landscapes from the point of view of the people we wish to understand, developing a comprehension for the 'native eye'. For example, wetlands have traditionally been seen as physically and socially marginal landscapes or as sources of economic benefit, but such a view belongs typically to the outsider.

In this chapter we also explore the role of wetlands, or certain wetland types and specific locales within them, as places that were storehouses of cultural and symbolic meaning. The enculturation of nature through inhabitation, whereby the perception of areas changed from wilderness to cultural landscape, may be particularly relevant for wetland studies. Certain wetlands became the foci of votive depositions, and concepts of liminality are frequently invoked when discussing wetlands, and thus the study of wetlands as 'natural places' will be discussed here (Bradley 2000). At the same time, we also need to recognise that some wetlands were part of the landscape of everyday life – that is, they were 'taskscapes' (Ingold 1993) – and this will be the final theme developed in this chapter. Throughout this chapter, we give examples of opportunities that arise to embrace high-resolution dating and detailed palaeoenvironmental data for reconsidering people's inter-relationship with nature.

The concept of wetlands: deconstructing the meta-narrative

Inventing and inventorying wetlands

It is most doubtful that people in the past ever thought about wetlands in the landscape in the ways we do today. Indeed, 'wetlands' as a word did not exist in the English language before the 1960s, nor were there equivalents in Dutch, Old Frisian, German, French or Danish. Ancient place-names that include the generic term wetland as a prefix or suffix are also non-existent, although the Dutch place-name Waterland comes close. Instead, we find plenty of English place-names (often deriving from Anglo-Saxon roots) indicating *specific* kinds of wet landscapes or wet features, with suffices such as -ings, -hay, -moor, -dyke, -fen, -levels, -fleet, -pool, -mere, -beach, -ford, -bridge, or -on-the-water and -on-the-Marsh. Similarly, in

2. Places in watery worlds

Irish, place-names often incorporate specific words for marshes (*corcach*), water meadows (*cluain*) and bogs (*móin*), but there is no word for wetlands. We have also plenty of other place-names that indicate the kind of wetness of specific locations, such as the evocative Dirtness and Reedness, both in the Humber Wetlands of England. So, if people in the past did not use the word wetland, when was it invented and what does it mean?

Although writers referred to 'wet land' (i.e. waterlogged ground) in the eighteenth and nineteenth centuries, one of the earliest published uses of the term 'wetland' was in *Scientific American* in 1965, and it was also used in *Nature* in 1969 (referring to wetland flora and fauna). Thence the term 'wetlands' emerged in the 1960s in the United States of America, largely as a growing concern about the habitat of birds and especially ducks, and led to a number of federal laws that used the term wetland as a generic term for such habitats. That the pressure for such laws came principally from the hunting lobby matters not, but it explains the early preoccupation with generic, rather than specific, wetland protection.

During the UNESCO-sponsored International Convention on Wetlands in Ramsar, Iran, in 1970, the 'formal' definition of wetlands was agreed as follows: 'Wetlands are areas of marsh, fen, peatland or water, whether natural or artificial, permanent or temporary, with water that is static or flowing, fresh, brackish or salt, including areas of marine water the depth of which at low tide does not exceed six metres.' Much debate has since been dedicated to redefining this definition of wetlands, and the Ramsar Bureau itself provides an exhaustive list of the many specific kinds of wetlands that are included under the Convention. Within three major groups, comprising Marine/Coastal Wetlands, Inland Wetlands and Man-made Wetlands, it identifies 41 types of wetlands, such as permanent shallow marine waters, seasonal/intermittent freshwater marshes/pools on inorganic soils, salt exploitation sites and canals and drainage channels. This division is primarily based on the ecological functions and benefits of these types of wetlands.

Bradley (2000) has suggested that people in the past did not think in terms of environmental systems or ecosystems (e.g. wetlands), but developed 'native ecologies' using their own terms to define specific topographical features or places (e.g. that lake, this marsh, etc.). We can assume, if this was the case, that people in the past living within and outside the wetlands would have understood these landscapes in terms of particular land-forms, rather than by using the broad, generic term 'wet-lands'. Rethought wetland archaeology should similarly deconstruct the concept of wetlands when attempting to understand how people in the past engaged with these landscapes, and develop an empathy for the characteristics of the many wetlands as seen and understood by the people we study.

Archaeology of diverse wetlands

It is evident that even in environmental terms, different types of wetland offer quite different resources for food gathering, the use of raw materials, potential for accessibility and for reclamation. This diversity of past wetlands and its implications for archaeological study has been explored by several scholars (e.g. Mitsch & Gosselink 1993; Dinnin & Van de Noort 1999). They have argued against the sweeping assertion that all wetlands offer attractive ecological conditions with a natural high bio-productivity and biodiversity. Indeed, in a calculation of the biomass generated in a range of wetland landscapes compared to non-wetland ecosystems, it was found that whilst certain wetlands are indeed amongst the most bio-productive ecosystems in the world, others belong to the poorest in terms of bio-productivity.

So, from a modern ecological perception, biogenic wetlands (that is the wetlands formed through the accumulation of peat, such as blanket bogs and raised mires) are wetlands with levels of biomass production that are among the lowest in the world. This is caused by saturation by rainwater, which deprives plants of nutrients and oxygen. They also have a low biodiversity, as only a limited number of specialised plants (e.g. *Sphagnum* mosses) can tolerate the high water table, acidity and low nutrient availability. The minerogenic wetlands (that is, wetlands formed primarily through the accumulation of silts and clays such as river floodplains and areas with marine sedimentation containing alder carrs, sedge fens and reed-swamps) have access to groundwater and floodwater, and so benefit from the water-borne nutrients brought into the ecosystem. Riverine wetlands that are regularly inundated by floodwaters from streams and rivers have an even higher primary productivity and greater biodiversity, and as nutrient levels in the water increase downstream, river deltas and estuaries are amongst the highest biomass producers in the world, with annelids, molluscs, fish and waterfowl feeding on plants, and thus contributing to a greater biodiversity.

Wetlands archaeological research in the Humber Basin has revealed interesting correlations in the distribution of archaeological sites and different types of wetlands in the past (see Dinnin & Van de Noort 1999; Van de Noort 2004b). From the earliest Mesolithic through to the high Middle Ages, many more sites were found in the Humber estuary and alongside the many rivers that flow into it, than in any of the peatlands of this region. Taking a broader overview of the published literature, it seems reasonable to suggest that features and sites thought to be related to food production or daily life were predominantly located on what were minerogenic wetlands.

Leendert Louwe Kooijmans' (1993) synthesis of research in the Dutch delta also makes it apparent that the majority of prehistoric sites in its wetlands were not located in what would have been peatlands, but near rivers and within minerogenic wetlands. Similarly, research on England's east coast, in the Fenlands of East Anglia, found many more prehistoric and Roman-period sites on the fen edges and alongside rivers than within the peat, although many sites were subsequently submerged by mires (Hall & J. Coles 1994; Hayes 1988). This accounts, to a considerable extent, for the fact that the overwhelming majority of the sites from these landscapes were frequently buried by subsequent alluvial deposits or peat, but were not themselves waterlogged. On the Severn estuary, most Bronze Age and Iron Age houses, dwellings and trackways were focused on the zone between the mires and the saltmarshes, attracted no doubt by the rich grazing of the minerogenic wetlands (Bell *et al.* 2000). Similarly, on the Shannon estuary, while there is evidence for prehistoric and medieval activity down by the estuarine marshes, there is rather less in the region's peatlands (O'Sullivan 2001). Finally, in the Roman period and the Middle Ages, both small- and large-scale reclamation and transformation of wetlands centred initially on alluvial wetlands, rather than the mires (e.g. Rippon 2000). The peatlands were, as a rule, the last type of wetlands to be reclaimed.

If we consider this diversity of wetland landscapes, and how this diversity would have been perceived by people in the past living within or outside the wetlands, it becomes apparent that the term wetland in interpretative studies is too broad. It forms an appropriate entity only in the sense that anoxic environments have caused the preservation of organic archaeological and palaeoenvironmental remains that require specialist methods and techniques during recovery and analysis. However, as has been so clearly shown in place-names, past people never thought about wetlands in the landscape generally, but instead considered the values, merits and dangers of specific types of wetlands. This should be taken fully into consideration both in studies focusing on the economical exploitation of specific wetland landscapes, and in those focusing on other aspects of prehistoric and historic societies.

The Humber Wetlands: different wetlands, different wetland archaeology

Recognising the fundamental differences in the many types of wetland landscapes and what people did there is an essential component of rethought wetlands. In the Humber Wetlands, for example, the dichotomy in types of activity in minerogenic wetlands and peatlands remains striking (Van de Noort 2004b). On the silts and clays in the Humber Wetlands, for example, archaeological survey has found few monumental sites, or types of sites traditionally associated with death and burial. Instead, the survey identified 'hunting camps' and 'flint production sites', field systems, settlements, and sites of industrial activities, including salt winning and metal production or, if one wishes, the archaeology of 'daily life'. The palynological evidence indicates something similar; the opening up of the indigenous forest throughout the Neolithic and Bronze Age, with little remaining woodland by the start of the Iron Age. In contrast, the archaeology of the peatlands of this region offers a dearth of settlements and field systems, and there is also a pronounced lack of finds of flint or pottery. Instead, the antiquarian finds of bog bodies from Thorne and Hatfield Moors in the Humberhead Levels, and a large number of Bronze Age and Iron Age bronze objects 'ritually deposited' in the moors and floodplain mires, testify to a perception that is strikingly different from that attributable to the minerogenic wetlands. The place-names still used in the region reflect this differential perception of the many types of wetlands. The alluvial or minerogenic wetlands are usually called 'sands', 'levels' or 'carrs', whereas the organic peatlands were known as 'moors' and 'wastes', and peatlands were thus understood to have been marginal landscapes.

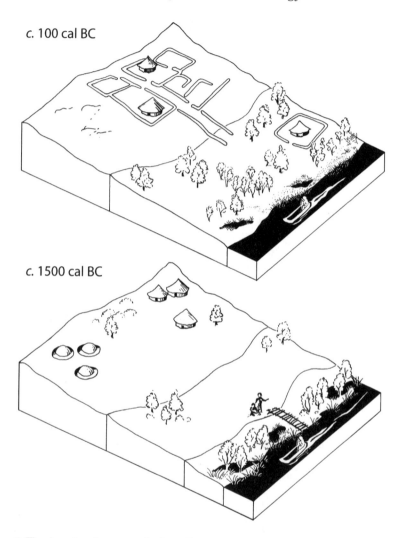

3. The changing character of a riverside wetland in the Humber basin, England, between 1500 and 100 cal BC, showing how the function and perception of wetlands changes over time. The 'votive deposition' of bronze artefacts around 1500 cal BC reflects such a time-specific perception of this expanding peatland; by 100 cal BC, a flood has left a minerogenic deposit which has changed the perception and use of this wetland (after Van de Noort 2004: 169).

2. Places in watery worlds

We must guard, however, against translating cultural- or contextual-specific observations into cross-cultural or non-contextualised generalisations. This is exactly what Rod Giblett set out to do in his *Postmodern Wetlands: Culture, History, Ecology* (1996), where he proposed a 'post-structuralist' distinction of the different types of wetlands, based on English literature. The 'white waters' (i.e. rivers and minerogenic wetlands) represent masculinity, culture, progress and development, the latter often under the direction of distant owners, authority and capital, whereas the 'dark pools' (i.e. peatlands) signify femininity, nature, stagnation, disease and opposition to progress and development.

Whilst the archaeology of the Humber Wetlands in the Bronze Age and Iron Age contains ample characteristics that underwrite aspects of this post-structuralist description, such an opposition is wholly untenable for the same area in the Roman and medieval periods, when the peatlands were extensively transformed and exploited, and peat itself became a valuable commodity as fuel. The reasons for their exploitation were economically, socially and politically determined, rather than intrinsically linked to the natural properties of the specific wetlands.

North Holland: perception of different wetlands

A study from the Netherlands may be used here to illustrate further the importance of cultural perceptions when considering the way in which people in the past perceived the different types of wetlands. The lowlands in North Holland had been exploited from the Neolithic onwards, but the late Roman and early medieval marine transgression, coupled with the erosion of the ancient dune system, provides an environmental reason for the discontinuation of settlement in this marginal landscape.

41

From the fifth to the eighth century AD this landscape remained largely devoid of human interference, as shown by the palynological record for the region and the dearth of archaeological sites and finds. However, from the ninth century AD onwards, archaeological sites including settlements appear within the peatlands. Whereas environmental factors, and especially a period of reduced rainfall, enabled this colonisation of the peatlands, the socio-political factors of the day are considered of greater importance.

Jan Besteman (1990, 117), in his study of the colonisation of the peatlands of North Holland, considers the early medieval socio-political context of patrons and clients. The king, occupying the top of the feudal pyramid, would have been perceived as the landowner of any wilderness such as the peatlands of North Holland. However, with the declining control of the Carolingian kings over their vassals after the middle of the ninth century, the latter usurped the peat bogs for themselves. Continuing erosion of political structures and increasing geographical distance between the seats of the local elites and the areas of reclamation in the subsequent centuries gave rise to groups of 'free' farmers. These 'free farmers' were no longer bound by oath, obligation or tax to their patrons, and these apparently marginal wetland landscapes had become fundamentally attractive places to live.

The concept of marginality has been invoked for many wetlands, in particular by archaeologists and historians not specialised in their study. As argued above, from an economic point of view it is certainly true that specific types of wetlands have lower bio-productivity than adjacent free-draining landscapes. Marginality, however, can only be understood fully as the interaction of economic and cultural factors. The examples used so far from North Holland and the Humber Wetlands illustrate this point.

Enculturing nature

Thus far, in the tradition of wetland archaeology over the last few decades, we have focused on the economic aspects of wetlands in the landscape. However, wetland landscapes were perceived in other ways as well, and much has been said and written about their most intriguing archaeological treasures: the bog bodies and wooden trackways. It has long been accepted that it is unlikely that people in our prehistoric past divided life up into segments, and that the economic, social, political and religious aspects of life were all, to varying degrees, interwoven. For this reason, one cannot translate the economic marginality of the peatlands directly into their role in ritualised behaviour, especially when considering those wetland types across different cultures or through time. Nevertheless, it is beyond doubt that different types of wetlands were perceived essentially differently within certain societies at particular points in time. For example, Jan Besteman's (1990, 117) description of the peatlands of North Holland in the early Middle Ages as 'a wilderness', discussed earlier, invokes images of an uninhabited or uninhabitable landscape, even though subsequent events showed that people could live there quite agreeably. In this section we look at some different perceptions of wetlands, and will consider how people engaged with them in terms of ritual behaviour, and in the process encultured the wetlands.

Star Carr – a Mesolithic ritual site?

The excavations and interpretations of Star Carr, in the Vale of Pickering in Yorkshire, are well documented. The excavations by Grahame Clark between 1949 and 1951 were initially published in 1954, and updated in 1972, with Star Carr described as a hunter-gatherer 'base camp', dated to *c.* 9500 BP.

A major reappraisal of the site's function was published by Robin Legge and Peter Rowley-Conwy in 1988, describing the site essentially as a seasonally occupied 'hunting camp', but alternative models and explanations have been proposed. Further research of the environmental context of the site was published in *Star Carr in Context*, edited by Paul Mellars and Petra Dark in 1998. Most recently, Chantal Conneller and Tim Shadla-Hall (2003) have considered twelve other Early Mesolithic sites in the Vale of Pickering, and conclude that Star Carr was an exceptional site, used in a variety of different ways by different people.

Clark's original work produced no less than 191 (unfinished) barbed points, but only one other has been found in the many years of work in the Vale of Pickering since 1975. Furthermore, the famous antler frontlets with perforated holes remain unique for the British Isles, if not in Europe. Additional finds such as the shale and amber beads, and the perforated teeth of red deer, have few parallels in the region. It could be argued that the antler barbed points and antler frontlets would not survive in anything but waterlogged deposits and that their absence on the other twelve Early Mesolithic sites in the Vale of Pickering is the result of differential survival, rather than differential deposition. However, this argument is rejected by Conneller and Shadla-Hall who consider the whole structure of deposition on the site to be markedly different from the other sites. An important component of their argument is a detailed analysis of the flint finds from the site, which shows that Star Carr, with its relative prevalence of burins which are considered to have been used in the manufacture of bone and antler objects, is in this respect also exceptional within the Vale of Pickering.

Conneller and Shadla-Hall (2003, 102-3) do not wish to redefine Star Carr as a 'ritual site', as this is considered too narrow, but they note that the range of artefacts from Star Carr makes this an atypical site within the contexts of the Vale of Pickering in the tenth millennium BP. The ritual aspects of Star Carr, and not dissimilar assemblages from Early Mesolithic sites such as Friesack in northern Germany, lead them to explain the site as a locale within the landscape that had been selected 'for the deposition of specific objects, particularly objects manufactured from animal remains' such as the barbed points, and 'a place where human and animal identities were explored and blurred'.

We may ask ourselves how important the wetland context of these finds was, and whether we must try to understand the site as one where an early form of 'votive deposition in wet places' was practised, as has been proposed for some of the Mesolithic wetlands in southern Scandinavia (Larsson 2001; see below for a discussion on this phenomenon in the Bronze Age). This is a tempting proposition. The presence of the half-finished barbed points has a resonance with the never-used bronze weapons and extremely thin bronze shields which find their way into selected wetlands as votive deposits in the Bronze Age across much of Europe (Bradley 1990), and this could represent one way of approaching votive depositions, alongside the practice of depositing used objects. The selection of this specific locale on the edge of Lake Pickering as a place for the deposition of objects makes it certainly one of the earliest sites where a wild wetland is encultured (see Zvelebil 2003).

The Neolithic Sweet Track, Somerset

A reappraisal of existing interpretations of the Sweet Track in the Somerset Levels may provide another fruitful avenue for considering the cognitive and ideological aspects of past societies. The Sweet Track has been introduced in Chapter 1. To date, excavators and commentators alike (e.g. B. & J. Coles 1986;

Edmonds 1999, 24) have argued that the track was built to connect two areas of dryland, the Polden Hills to the north and Westhay island to the south, for reasons of contact, exchange and trade (although a recent paper by Bond 2004 also considers the Sweet Track in the context of spirituality).

Alongside the track, various objects were recovered during the excavations. Amongst these were a polished jadeite axe from central Europe, unhafted and in pristine condition, flint arrowheads and axes, pottery, yew pins, a broken pot filled with hazelnuts, a fragment of a bow, an arrow shaft, a wooden bowl and an object that has been interpreted as a child's toy axe of oak, but which may alternatively be seen as a (votive) token. The pollen record for the region shows the impact of woodland clearance or management, possibly associated with the construction of the Sweet Track, but it also indicates subsequent woodland regeneration or regrowth, rather than the expansion of agriculture.

In a popular reconstruction drawing of the track by Edward Mortelmans, we see a man, a child and a woman walking along the track, presumably a family on its way to visit kin across the wetlands. The track is set within the reed swamp, but the reeds either side of the track have been cut just above the water. The man carries a hafted polished flint axe, a bag and a bow and arrows; one of the birds overhead could be his next prey. The boy carries a wooden axe, the woman a wooden pot. From a gender archaeology perspective, the reconstruction drawing can be critiqued (Joanna Brück, pers. comm.): the hirsute man actively strides out, forcefully in front, the woman passively walks behind with the child, her breasts modestly covered, as she holds her 'handbag' by her side. In any case, this is a reconstruction of a Neolithic nuclear family going about some relatively prosaic task, on a shopping trip to the bountiful 'wetlands' perhaps. In a sense, the reconstruction drawing is very symptomatic of how we make sense of the past, and

4. Reconstruction of the Sweet Track, Somerset, England (drawn by Edward Mortlemans; courtesy of the Somerset Levels Project/Somerset County Council).

condensed everything we know about the track during its ten-year use into a single moment.

Explanations to date have not given any thought to Neolithic people's perception and experience of this wetland in the wider landscape, and this results in an exclusively utilitarian outlook on the Sweet Track itself. Let us reconsider the track and its context. Even within a functionalist paradigm, it is worth pointing out that the Westhay 'island' had nothing to offer in terms of exploitable resources that could not be found on the Polden Hills and *vice versa*, and the wetland-dryland interface could be readily exploited (e.g. for wood, reeds and herbs) from all along the edge of either of these dryland areas. The use of the 'other side' as pasture land is possible, but the track certainly would not have been passable for cattle or sheep. This raised footpath allowed people a dry passage, but it would have been quite difficult to pass oncoming travellers (without becoming rather intimate), and outright impossible whilst carrying any large loads such as reeds or wood. Using the track to exploit the wetlands, for example for fowling, is also doubtful as the hunter would have had to leave the track to recover the kill. A logboat would be more suitable for such activity, and such a craft could also conveniently have been used to maintain contacts between kin groups in the Somerset Levels and for the exchange of goods. The construction of a logboat or curachs (or even several logboats) would have been achieved at a fraction of the labour and timber cost required for the construction of the Sweet Track, and the track itself would have been a barrier to logboats.

The excavators of the Sweet Track, John and Bryony Coles, have always recognised that the artefacts found alongside it may either (or variously) have been dropped accidentally or placed in the reed swamp on (ritual) purpose (e.g. B. Coles 1999). Considering the material culture of the Neolithic in Somerset, and particularly the presence of the exotic jade axe alongside the Sweet Track, the latter of the two explanations must be favoured. The practice of votive deposition of a range of objects in 'wet places' from the Mesolithic through to the post-medieval period in much of western Europe have been described in outline elsewhere (e.g. Bradley 1990, 2000), and it is probable that the jade axe and the other objects including the bowl with hazelnuts and wooden child's axe form part of this tradition.

If the Sweet Track was not a trackway to the food store or the practical solution to a traveller's inconvenience it has been claimed to be, than we should explore alternative explanations. In our view, both the wooden structure itself and the artefacts alongside the Sweet Track underpin the notion that early Neolithic people saw this wetland as a landscape with clear symbolic meaning, and possibly as a 'wilderness'. Within the context of the early Neolithic of south-west England, the Sweet Track remains unique in its early date, construction and length, and as a functional site it is something of an anomaly. Like their contemporaries in other parts of south-west England, the community that built and used the track was one of predominantly pastoral farmers who continued to hunt and gather foodstuffs, and may have been of no fixed abode. Living in temporary lodges in clearings, rather than in long-term settlements with long houses, much of their collective energy was expended on the construction of monuments, such as long barrows and causewayed enclosures. Within this interpretative framework, the importance and significance of such monuments have been explained in terms of offering fragmented and dispersed communities opportunities to trade, exchange and reinforce kinship bonds through communal ceremonies linked to shared ancestry. Such monuments also offered kin groups a sense of place and, increasingly over time, a concept of ownership and ties with the land (Bradley 1998; Edmonds 1999).

If such a view of early Neolithic society and settlement is accepted, should the extraordinary amount of energy and timber used for the Sweet Track be seen as a monumental building aimed, as many other cultural markers of this period, at essentially creating a sense of place? Christopher Tilley (1994) has argued that tracks and paths are primary human artefacts. They were one of the first modifications people made to their environment, forming a medium through which the environment could be integrated with the psyche and transformed into a landscape, that is, an environment which reflects and is interpreted by human beings. The environment thus becomes 'encultured' into landscape (Tilley 1994, 206-7). The concepts of paths and roads, and the journeys that they enable, are powerful metaphors (Tilley 1999, 178), recognised by the Romans and even by us in our modern, so-called rational culture. Thus the path is not just a route from one place to another, but more importantly, it transforms a wilderness full of unknowns into a cultured landscape, a known place. The deposition of artefacts reinforces this symbolic role of the Sweet Track (e.g. B. & J. Coles 1986). We could postulate that the depositions represent occasions, over the ten years in which the track may have been used, when this symbolic function was reinforced.

If early Neolithic society in south-west England was of a more sedentary nature than can currently been demonstrated archaeologically, we could consider alternative explanations for the Sweet Track. For example, the track may have acted as a boundary, between two social groups. Or the island of Westhay may have been perceived as an area with special, ritual meaning, a 'natural' place in Richard Bradley's (2000) definition, with the Sweet Track providing access for pilgrimages.

Trackways from the Bourtanger Moor, Netherlands

Other trackways built elsewhere in Europe have been similarly reinterpreted as functioning at the same time in profane and sacred spheres. Several trackways in the raised mires of Drenthe, in the eastern part of the Netherlands, and adjacent Lower Saxony in Germany, have been dated to the Neolithic period (e.g. Casparie 1987). Probably the best-known of these is the Nieuw-Dordrecht trackway, dated through radiocarbon assay to *c.* 2900-2450 cal BC. New dating evidence using dendro-chronology combined with wiggle-matching of radiocarbon dates has shown that the track was constructed in phases, with at one point a gap of a century in activity. Constructed from roundwood timbers, and in places positioned over longitudinally positioned timbers, it extends for nearly one kilometre into the Bourtanger Moor from a sand ridge known as the Hondsrug, with a width of 2.5 to 3 metres. The abrupt 'end' of the trackway somewhere in the Bourtanger Moor has occasioned much debate. Suggestions that the trackway was constructed to enable the exploitation of the bog ore for iron production have been dismissed on the grounds that iron production did not commence for at least another two millennia. Similarly, it is unlikely that the building project was abandoned because the people involved in its construction were insufficiently familiar with the landscape. Wijnand Van der Sanden (2001, 141-2) argues instead for a ritual function for this trackway. He points to the artefacts that have been deposited beneath or near the trackway as evidence: the wooden disc wheel, the axe handle, the 'hockey stick', and the cache of flint, which included one axe and eleven long blades.

We could speculate that the phased extension of the Nieuw-Dordrecht trackway was intended to access new areas of (unspoilt) wilderness, whilst the repeated building of extensions would also have played an important role in reinforcing socio-political relations. Existing parts of the track, and any associated votive depositions that had taken place there, had effectively encultured those parts of the Bourtanger Moor. To communicate with the ancestors, ghosts or gods that resided in untainted nature, or to domesticate un-encultured areas of the bog, the track had to be extended periodically. In this manner, wetlands were encultured through ritualised activities such as the deposition of bodies in bog pools and of bronze artefacts at the edge of expanding peatlands – and, one might suggest, through the construction of trackways, beliefs and myths (e.g. Tilley 1994).

Van der Sanden (2001, 143) reinterprets another trackway from the Bourtanger Moor, the Valtherbrug, now dated by wiggle-matching of radiocarbon and dendrochronological dates to the first century AD, as a non-utilitarian road. This 12 km (!) long trackway links an area of known occupation, the Hondsrug, with one that wasn't occupied, the Westerwolde. Palaeoenvironmental analysis shows that the region became increasingly wet, and that the Westerwolde area was not farmed. Finds from near the track included four bog bodies, all more or less contemporary with the track, at least five querns, and wagons or parts of wagons. Van der Sanden suggests that the track was used for ritual processions. Rather than periodically extending the track, as was the case with the Nieuw-Dordrecht trackway, the function of the Valtherbrug lay in recurrent ceremonies.

Bronze Age and Iron Age trackways and causeways

In the Irish Midlands, the number of trackways linking areas of dry ground across the extensive raised mires are numerous, and range in date from the Neolithic through to the post-medieval era (Raftery 1996). The frequent rebuilding of tracks on the same alignment have to date been explained only functionally, that is that the new trackways were constructed to maintain contact in periods of climatically induced rapid upward growth of the peat. Alternatively or concurrently, it could be suggested that the trackways were built at least in part as a way of enculturing the raised mire. The more dynamic the raised mire, the greater its association with metaphysical phenomena in the eyes of people who lived within it or nearby. Domesticating such dynamic landscapes became a matter of urgency when periods of increased wetness resulted in accelerated peat growth and an advance of the wilderness areas through the burial of whole trackways. Dated to 148 BC by dendrochronology, the spectacular Iron Age Corlea 1 trackway, the largest of the Irish trackways, has already been interpreted as a structure with political, social and ideological functions (Raftery 1996). Its massive design and its apparent deliberate disassembly towards the middle of the route suggest that the track may have had a similar symbolic function to other major trackways, but the project involved a larger number of people, possibly under the leadership of a local chief, and was executed in a most impressive fashion.

Many trackways from other regions are associated with human remains and gold and bronze artefacts, suggesting a ritual or symbolic role alongside a vernacular one. At Islandmagrath on the Fergus estuary, a Late Bronze Age wooden trackway was located near the findspot of a gold bracelet (O'Sullivan 2001, 125-8). On the Crouch estuary in Essex, a Late Bronze Age wooden causeway was associated with two seemingly deliberately placed human skulls (Wilkinson & Murphy 1995). It is not conceptually hard to link these smaller structures with the larger Bronze Age and Iron Age timber causeways found at Testwood Lakes, Eton Rowing Lakes, the River Thames (Vauxhall), Caldicot and Fiskerton, all of which appear to have been routes out into watery worlds, associated with the deposition of human remains, weapons, ornaments and pottery.

The significance of trackways in enculturing selected wetlands may be summarised as follows. Certain wetland landscapes are not ordinary places. Peatlands such as raised mires can be treacherous to cross. They offer a constantly changing geography with no permanent landmarks. They are associated with unusual phenomena, such as spontaneous ignition of methane. They can be neither cultivated nor easily used for pasture (but see below). Their fabric is neither stone nor soil, and anyone who has inadvertently stepped onto a quaking bog will know that it is neither land nor water. Bogs are thus dangerous, disorientating, enigmatic and otherworldly places which are resistant to domestication, save by draining. Domestication of the environment is deeply significant to an agrarian society such as existed in Neolithic and Bronze Age Europe (e.g. Bradley 1993). To these people, bogs, in their truculent wildness, would have appeared possessed of a power which opposed domestication, and thus opposed their culture. This power therefore needed to be acknowledged and, perhaps, placated (Adam Wainwright pers. comm.). Of course, such a process of enculturation would have been reinforced by the everyday use of the trackways, and the ritual and everyday aspects would have continually reinforced each other.

In describing how people thought about certain wetland landscapes, such as the Somerset Levels, the peatlands of North Holland, the raised mire of Bourtanger Moor, and the peatlands of the Irish Midlands, the concept of 'wilderness' may be useful. Wilderness is a landscape-construct formed by human perception and imagination (Cosgrove 1984, 11). It has been argued that for many societies world-wide, wilderness is the perceived place of origin of distant ancestors, or is sensed as that part of the landscape where natural or social rebirth and regeneration takes place (e.g. Oelschlaeger 1991; Cosgrove 1993, 291). The concept of wilderness was also used to define boundaries that could not be crossed. For certain wetland landscapes, a role such as wilderness is archaeologically demonstrated by a number of late prehistoric bog bodies and votive depositions. Wijnand van der Sanden (1996) entitled his book on bog bodies in Europe *Through Nature to Eternity*, expressing his understanding of this phenomenon: the bog pools that received the bodies connected this world with the next and enabled the regeneration of this world. Mires are therefore frequently associated with supernatural powers, a notion that was reinforced by their constantly changing geography.

Boundaries and edges: wetlands as natural places

Marginality and liminality

It would be mistaken to assume that landscapes that were places of work (i.e. of economic exploitation) were by definition non-ritual landscapes or, conversely, to assume that ritual and symbolic landscapes had no economic value at all. We have already argued that the mires that were perceived as other-worldly landscapes could be encultured, and thus that their economic 'exploitation' could have been enabled. The example of the early medieval inhabitation of the space previously regarded as 'wilderness' in North Holland shows how perceptions of landscapes were transformed with socio-political change, and many peatlands across the world have become resources for peat as fuel, bedding for domestic animals, and for mulch in the horticultural industry. We must, in addition, accept that specific locales within certain types of wetlands seem to have been chosen for ritualised activities. Although the ritual activities themselves effectively encultured such locales (Tilley 2001), their long-term use shows that their importance as places where one could communicate with nature, or with the gods, ancestors or ghosts, was retained over long periods of time. We do accept, however, that the meaning of such places changed with every ritual activity that took place there. Such locales could be termed 'natural places', as argued by Richard Bradley (2000).

Recent research in the Witham valley in Lincolnshire, England, offers an outstanding example of the longevity of the significance of some natural places in wetlands. Stocker and Everson (2003) studied this lowland valley running from the vicinity of the town of Lincoln towards the coastal region of the Wash. In the Middle Ages, the River Witham was the boundary of the independent state of Lindsey. Research found that the medieval monasteries were located at strategic points along the valley where causeways provided access across the river and its extensive riparian wetlands. In the Middle Ages the causeways were already of great age, and excavations of one of them, at Fiskerton, showed a predecessor of Iron Age and Roman date (Field & Parker Pearson 2003). The causeways were also associated with votive depositions, which occur in this area only at the terminals of the causeways. In turn, these votive depositions were found to be in the vicinity of Bronze Age barrow cemeteries. Stocker and Everson (2003) thus argue that specific locales within the Witham valley were perceived as places where one could cross this boundary for a period in excess of two millennia, despite the evolving nature of this wetland landscape. Bronze Age perceptions endured, in one way or another, into the Middle Ages, with the medieval monasteries effectively Christianising pagan practices and beliefs.

The concept of liminality is frequently invoked where wetlands are traversed. Liminality, a notoriously fluid concept, is linked to 'rites of passage', originally proposed by Van Gennep (1906) to describe the formalised rituals and practices that accompany one's transition from one particular state into another, especially the rites associated with birth, reaching adulthood, marriage and death. As part of these rituals, symbolic or real 'thresholds' needed to be crossed, with the thresholds constituting liminal zones. This concept seems applicable in the case of the Witham – crossing this boundary was evidently some sort of rite of passage accompanied by specific rituals.

As economic and ritual activities are not, on a landscape level, mutually exclusive, the recurrent equation of liminality with marginality is similarly mistaken. Although some liminal zones were to be found in what were considered marginal landscapes, others (e.g. the threshold passed by newlyweds in the modern world) are located within settlements or within areas in economic use. In other words we must be very specific when identifying places that were liminal.

The manifestation of liminality in wetlands can come in different guises. Francis Pryor (1988) argues that the Neolithic causewayed enclosure at Etton, near Maxey in the East Anglian Fenlands, was used for rites of passage related to transitions after death. The location of the site, on the boundary of wetland and dryland, stresses its liminality. Equally, the deposition of bronze weapons and artefacts alongside the Flag Fen causeway is interpreted as relating to rites of passage and, therefore, the causeway and its setting are interpreted as a liminal space. A reappraisal of the so-called West Furze lake-dwellings, in Yorkshire, showed that the site was in effect a Neolithic trackway across a mire that had developed in the Bail and Low Mere complex (Van de Noort 1995). These elongated mires may have been seen as a boundary between the world of the living and the world of the dead, with evidence of two burial mounds to the east of the former meres, and somewhat tentatively a settlement on their west bank. The trackway at West Furze that crossed these wetlands included several features that could have symbolised this liminal space, most notably the wicket or doorway at the eastern terminal of the short trackway. The symbolic function of this boundary was further reinforced with a number of human skulls.

Votive depositions in wet places

The most significant phenomenon that could possibly be considered as signifying some aspect of liminality in wetlands, and undoubtedly as a practice associated with natural places, is the 'votive deposition in wet places' described by Richard Bradley in his influential *Passage of Arms* (1990). He provides a long-term overview of this pan-European practice, and describes votive depositions in wet places as 'Gifts to the Gods' (see Gregory 1980), with clear socio-political and economic functions. Currently, the notion of 'votive deposition' requires reconsideration within the broader concept of 'structured deposition', recognising that certain cosmological rules governed the discarding and disposal of artefacts, human remains and rubbish that has been observed for much of the European Bronze Age and Iron Age (e.g. Hill 1995).

The term 'wet places' calls to mind the problems of using the term 'wetlands' that we discussed earlier in this chapter. Bradley (1990) concentrated his research on areas with particularly high densities of bronze votive depositions, such as the Thames valley, but this reliance on evidence that has been accumulated over several centuries has resulted in the environmental context of many finds not being considered. Others have also argued that water and wetlands were used for votive depositions on the grounds that they were places that were life-giving for all organisms and where contact with the metaphysical world was possible (e.g. Larsson 2001), but the lack of specificity in their arguments as to particular locations masks important aspects of the votive deposition in wet places.

In fact, many votive depositions seem to have been associated with places where waters or wetlands were crossed. To return to an earlier example, Stocker and Everson (2003) argued that the votive deposition in the Witham valley in the prehistoric period was linked geographically to the Iron Age causeways. Similarly, Davey (1973) identified the natural constriction in the Ancholme valley at Brigg, also in Lincolnshire, as a place of high concentration for votive deposition. That this location was used for cross-river and cross-wetland transport is exemplified by three Bronze Age finds from the same area: the Brigg 'raft', the Brigg logboat and the Brigg trackway. A similar argument can be made for Flag Fen, with the causeway providing a crossing from Fengate to Northey, and possibly the Sweet Track.

More importantly, another feature that many sites have in common is that the votive deposition of objects did not involve their being thrown into the water, but nearly always being carefully placed in shallow water. Where votive deposits have been excavated by archaeologists, this is almost always true. It is the case for Mesolithic flint caches in Sweden (e.g. Larsson 2001), for the Neolithic pots in Denmark (Koch 1999), probably for the jade axe, the bowl with hazelnuts and the child's axe near the Sweet Track (B. & J. Coles 1986), for the wooden wheels beneath the Nieuw-Dordrecht Trackway (Van der Sanden 2001), for the deposition of bronze artefacts and whole pots in the Wissey embayment in the East Anglian Fenlands (Healey 1996), the bronze weapons at Flag Fen (Pryor 2001) and even the Nydam and Hjortspring boats in Denmark (Crumlin-Pedersen & Munch Thye 1995), to name only a selection of well-known but highly diverse finds and sites. The subsequent extension of the wetland, for example under the influence of sea-level rise, enveloped these artefacts in peat, thus creating the impression that these were bog deposits. One can wonder whether the dynamic nature of wetlands reinforced the perception that these landscapes were in some way alive and thus home to supernatural powers. To achieve this careful deposition, the person doing the offering would have had to stand in the water himself, thus gaining a certain intimacy with the water and the supernatural, which may not have been available to any onlookers standing along the water's edge.

Wetlands as taskscapes

Notwithstanding our discussion of the non-utilitarian functions of trackways, their construction served practical purposes as well: to provide access across areas of otherwise impassable ground. Indeed, the ritual or special significance of trackways for the process of enculturation, as boundaries, or for rites of passages, was greatly enhanced by their use in everyday life. There is ample palaeoenvironmental evidence that the estuarine wetlands of the Thames (Meddens 1996), Humber (Van de Noort & Ellis 1999), Severn (Bell *et al.* 2000) and Shannon (O'Sullivan 2001), as well as many of those on the Somerset Levels (e.g. Tinney's Tracks; B. & J. Coles 1986), had economic or functional uses, for example to provide access for people or to allow cattle to utilise saltmarshes as seasonal feeding grounds, and formed part of the routine activities of daily life. In this section, we return to this theme in the study of wetlands as 'taskscapes'. This phrase was coined by Tim Ingold (1993) to focus on the concept that the manner in which landscapes are experienced and perceived is closely related to the activities or tasks that are undertaken in particular landscapes at particular times. This theme is further developed in Chapter 3, which considers the social identity of the people who worked and lived in the wetland.

The Irish Midlands bogs: trackways in wetland
'vernacular' landscapes?

Some wetlands were used as places for hunting, fowling or other relatively prosaic domestic activities. Until the 1990s, those trackways or toghers (from the Irish word *tóchar* for road) that had been identified in Ireland's Midlands bogs were interpreted as structures that crossed or spanned the entire wetlands. Stanley (2003, 65) has suggested that this led to a perception of bogs as wastelands, as obstacles to travel, and to a view of the large trackways as being on regional communication routeways. In fact, it now seems that the massive trackways such as the Iron Age road at Corlea 1, or the other substantial causeways in that bog that cross it (e.g. the Early Bronze Age track at Corlea 6 and the Late Bronze Age timber trackway at Derryoghill 1) are the abnormal ones (Raftery 1990, 1996). It is now known that large linear causeways that traverse a bog from one edge to another represent a very small proportion of the total number of known sites (McDermott 1998, 7; Stanley 2003, 65).

Recent archaeological surveys by the Irish Archaeological Wetland Unit have revealed that most of the three thousand wooden structures recorded in Irish Midland bogs to date are in fact short, narrow pathways or platforms constructed of hurdles, poles or bundles of brushwood (Stanley 2003). These indicate activity on the surface of the bog itself, rather than an attempt to cross it, and encourage 'a richer interpretative outlook in which bogs were part of everyday life for many people in the past and at different times would have represented a resource, a boundary, a barrier/refuge or a sacred place' (Stanley 2003, 65). Although raised bogs are not as resource-rich as minerogenic wetlands, they could have accommodated some hunting and fowling, and the gathering of some plants for medicinal purposes, crafts and building, while also providing turf for fuel. Raised bogs can also be used intermittently for short-term seasonal grazing by burning the top layer of the bog, for the preservation of butter, the seasoning of wood and the curing of leather. We should recognise that these activities, though seemingly economic practices, are things that people do every day, albeit in specific cultural and social conditions.

At Derryville Bog, Co. Tipperary, in southern Ireland, a major multidisciplinary project explored the archaeology and environment of a small raised mire from the Neolithic to the

Middle Ages. It revealed that the bog was used across time, and that it could be regarded as a 'vernacular landscape, a place for everyday life and practice in fens and marginal woodlands, rather than a supernatural boundary for ritual structured deposits' (Cross *et al.* 2000; O'Neill 2000). Naturally, such a perception of Derryville Bog depends on who made it, and the differences of the insider-outsider perspective is further explored in Chapter 3.

In the Middle Bronze Age (1700-1200 BC) a settlement of roundhouses was located on the dry ground at the margins of the bog. There was also a substantial cemetery of 28 cremation burials with pottery, frequently marked by wooden posts. In the wet margins at the edge of the wetlands, *fulachta fiadh* or burnt mounds were built for long-term use, for cooking, bathing, processing skins and undoubtedly many other activities. There were also short, narrow trackways constructed in wet parts of the fens and woodlands, seemingly as the result of casual low-level activities as people sought access out into the wetlands. There were a few larger stone causeways, narrow but relatively monumental, which crossed the entire bog. However, most structures aimed to merely bridge watery pools between drier parts of the bog's surface.

In the Late Bronze Age and Iron Age, wooden causeways, platforms and hurdles were also constructed in a casual way, often poorly constructed or not secured to the bog's surface with vertical wooden stakes. Many of these may have been used for brief periods of not more than twenty years. There were occasional larger structures, such as the timber causeway at Cooleeny 31, which may indeed have been on a regional network of movement through the raised mires of Templetuohy and Littleton. In the Iron Age, the dominant environment was a raised bog at the centre of the basin, but most human activities were focused on the watery fens and alder carr woodlands around the edges of the mire. By the early Middle Ages (i.e. AD

650-1250), hut sites and trackways may reveal an increasing activity, perhaps even inhabitation, on the surface of the raised bog itself, while waterlogged and unsafe locations within the bog seem to have been demarcated by rows of stakes.

However, in contrast with some of the Dutch, English and Irish bogland landscapes discussed above, this was not a place for power or high-status activities. In the Late Bronze Age and Iron Age, there is no archaeological evidence for high-status settlements in the vicinity (e.g. hillforts, or marsh-forts such as Sutton Common in England; see Chapter 5), nor is there any evidence for the deposition of high status metalwork or human remains in the bog itself. Interestingly, as revealed by the detailed palaeoenvironmental and archaeological studies, the local communities also showed a sensitivity to, and intimate knowledge of, the local environment, responding to different waterlogged conditions and bog bursts. The Derryville Bog sites can thus be interpreted as the wetland components of a broader 'vernacular landscape'. This landscape was a place for inhabitation, daily travel and movement, perhaps including various activities on the surface of the bog, but nonetheless no doubt incorporating sacred spaces and ritual behaviour.

Conclusion

This chapter has explored opportunities to study wetlands as landscapes from the point of view of the people we study. By 'empathising' with their actions and thoughts, approaching archaeological data from the point of view of past people's perceptions, by developing a feel for the 'native eye', and by being more explicit about our own modern preconceptions, new ways of understanding wetlands come within reach. This includes a more detailed appreciation of the diversity of types of landscapes than is encapsulated in the generic term 'wetland', and a more informed understanding about the range of values of specific types of wetland landscapes to people in the past. These values were always diverse, differing from time to time and from place to place, and everyday and sacred aspects of the landscape were always intertwined. This intertwining of values has been demonstrated in a number of case studies from Ireland, the UK and the Netherlands, exploring such concepts as wilderness, enculturation, liminality, marginality and taskscapes.

People of the wetlands? Exploring social identity in wetland archaeology

Introduction

Traditionally, wetland archaeologists have thought about their work as something that brings us closer to people of the past than is possible in 'dryland' archaeology (e.g. B. & J. Coles 1989; Raftery 1996). It is easy to see why this has happened. On wetland archaeological sites, there have been startling discoveries of Mesolithic human footprints in estuarine mudflats; Neolithic birch-bark chewing gum with a child's teeth marks; Bronze Age toolmarks on posts that even show traces of the tiny nicks in the cutting edges of blades and Iron Age bog bodies with beard-stubbled chins, intact fingernails and stomach contents revealing the last meals of executed victims (including Tollund Man, spectrally present on the cover of this book). It is certainly true that such discoveries generate a sense of wonder and excitement, providing a sense of a physical and emotional contact with other human beings from so long ago who have left such fragile, perishable traces, seemingly miraculously preserved.

However, other archaeologists have taken a different view and have noted that the people described in wetland archaeological publications were strangely the same the world over, and indeed across time. Tilley (1991), while allowing that wetland archaeology can indeed provide us with startling arrays of empirical evidence, noted that in some wetland archaeological texts there was little sense of people as social beings. As we have seen in Chapter 1, the 'people of the wetlands', he complained, seem to be regarded as simply 'bodies requiring tools, shelter, clothing and full stomachs of fish and fowl'. In his opinion, there was little attempt to explore how 'people of the wetlands' constructed distinctive social worlds through material forms.

Indeed, we also perhaps need to be more reflective about the classic phrase: 'people of the wetlands'. Is it possible that wetland archaeologists have uncritically bought into the historical (e.g. seventeenth- and eighteenth-century) representations of communities who live and work in wetlands, bogs and marshes as the classic anthropological 'other'? In many books and articles, the 'people of the wetlands' are portrayed as a bit wild and rebellious, ruggedly individualist, highly skilled and resourceful and living in ways that were culturally distinctive. Sometimes this was so. But it is worth remembering that such images are disturbingly similar to most colonial or 'outsider' representations of all people 'at the edge', as can be seen for example in the Classical authors' descriptions of Iron Age 'Celts' or English imperialist writings about the 'wild Irish' of nineteenth-century Ireland (James 1999). Thus we need to be careful when we think and write about people who inhabit and work in wetlands, and the wider worlds in which they lived.

In this chapter we will discuss the people of the wetlands, but in a different way. We will explore how people in the past (from communities to households to individuals) used their place, material culture and daily practice in wetlands to construct and negotiate distinctive social identities within broader worlds. We will discuss how wetland archaeology demonstrates how social identities were constructed and *performed* through the relationships between people, places, objects, animals and times, often at the edge of society, on physical and environmental boundaries or at places that were often socially and ideologically liminal. Recognising that places and landscapes are essential in defining identity, and indeed may have been perceived as active agents (see Chapter 2), we will also explore how wetlands worked on people, shaped their sense of self, and did things to them. We will look at archaeologies of settlement, fishing and landscape reclamation in particular, but we would argue that similar approaches can also be made to a wide range of wetland archaeological evidence.

Social identity: theory and practice in archaeology

It might be useful to discuss first how wetland archaeologists might now think about peoples who inhabit, move through and work in bogs, marshlands, fens and other watery places. Particularly inspiring is the increasing interest in identity in archaeology (e.g. Meskell 2001; Frazer & Tyrrell 2000). Social identity is usually defined as being about the ideas and knowledge that people had about their similarity and difference to others, thus providing people with information on how to 'get on', how to live and interact with each other; and the concept of identity is an important concept in postmodern sociology and anthropology.

The two sections below discuss the construction of social identities by and for people *living* in wetlands, the 'true' people of the wetlands, and by and for people *working* in wetlands. This separation is, obviously, not a reflection of reality, as people living in wetlands also work there, but is used here to draw out the different ways in which social identities can be formed and studied in wetland archaeology.

Living in wetland landscapes and social identities

It is clear that people in the past built, inhabited and lived in dwellings and landscapes in such a way as to construct and negotiate social identities of ethnicity, social class, gender, age and kinship, amongst other things. People, households and local communities constituted and expressed their social identities by ordering those worlds in which they lived. People also actively performed these social identities through the manipulation of material culture: their clothes, personal jewellery, hairstyles, the food they ate, the objects they used and their religious practices.

Some recent writings on social identity in archaeology have interpreted it in terms of some 'structuring principles', such as ethnicity, race, political organisation, kinship, gender, age, sexuality, the body, social class, ranking and role (Frazer & Tyrell 2000). Indeed, most recent perspectives on social identity emphasise such differences or boundaries, and tend to separate humans into distinct cultures, communities or social groups. We do always need to think about people as living within particular cultural and historical communities, and that they lived, worked and moved through landscapes as the men and women of these particular societies. However, it should also be possible to go further and explore other aspects of identity. We could think about how people used their 'sense of place' (e.g. an identification with locality, region and landscape), their knowledge of traditions and practices, their collective memories, senses of ancestry and understanding of history, imagined or otherwise, and their daily, practical engagement with dynamic, changing environments to construct and negotiate distinctive social identities. Furthermore, following Tilley's (2004, 222) recent suggestion, we might also think about wetlands as being active agents in the creation of people's sense of identity. This recent position is perhaps not all that far from one adopted by John and Bryony Coles in *People of the Wetlands* (1989), where they argued that the wetland landscapes played a formative role in how people organised themselves and expressed their identities.

3. People of the wetlands?

Early medieval crannogs and the 'performance' of social ranking

In the Bronze Age, Iron Age and the early Middle Ages (AD 400-1200) in Scotland and Ireland, people often built and lived on small islands of stone, earth and wood situated in the watery shallows of lakes. These islands, known today as crannogs, are amongst the most remarkable and evocative features of both the Scottish and the Irish archaeological landscapes and are perhaps the best-known aspects of Ireland's wetland archaeological heritage (e.g. B. & J. Coles 1989; O'Sullivan 1998, 2000, 2001b, 2001c; Fredengren 2002). Since the nineteenth century in Ireland, they have been the subject of antiquarian investigation (e.g. Wood-Martin 1886), while the archaeological excavation of crannogs such as Ballinderry Nos 1 and 2 (Hencken 1936, 1942) and Lagore (Hencken 1950) were formative events in the development of Irish archaeology (O'Sullivan 2003a). More recently, multidisciplinary excavations of sites such as Moynagh Lough (Bradley 1991) and Sroove (Fredengren 2001, 2002) have revealed good evidence for their houses, pathways, palisades, middens and the debris of domestic activity and craft production. Recent archaeological surveys have also indicated a surprising diversity of age, size, morphology, siting and location.

Ireland's early medieval crannogs have traditionally been interpreted as defensive refuges occupied at times of danger, or as high-status lake dwellings used for social display and prestige (e.g. Warner 1994; O'Sullivan 1998, 2000). However, it has also recently been established through the excavation of smaller crannogs such as Bofeenaun, Co. Mayo (Keane 1995), that many were seasonal or temporary occupation sites used for specialist crafts, particularly iron-working, while most sites may have been like Sroove, Co. Sligo: the lake-shore dwellings of the poor, landless or unfree (Fredengren 2002).

It is possible to explore how early medieval crannogs, as

islands on water, were used to construct and negotiate social identities within the community. In the early medieval imagination, islands were often seen as places apart, distant and enigmatic, located in a liminal space between land and water, between this world and the otherworld. The Irish annals frequently associate crannogs with violence and depict them as places that could be built, fortified and inhabited, destroyed by fire, looted and sacked by raiders on boats and overwhelmed by winter storms and floods. In the ninth-twelfth century AD hagiographies, saints frequently confront and defeat powerful individuals, usually kings, on their crannogs or defeat monsters on lake islands. Early medieval narrative literature, particularly ninth-/tenth-century voyage tales and adventure tales, also commonly depicts islands as fantastic, otherworldly places, so that heroes often go out onto magical lake islands, eat sumptuous feasts within fantastic houses there, fight battles and negotiate in various ways with otherworldly women.

There is a strong sense then of the different ways that islands were used to establish and structure different types of social identity, particularly in terms of social status, gender, e.g. the male patrimony of islands, and kinship. By inhabiting distant islands, by travelling to them by boat, or by negotiating with others upon them, the community's leaders, whether they be kings, saints or other male figures, were often depicted as having an ability to confront otherworldly forces to the benefit of the community. Of course, such early medieval texts were ideologically loaded, with the agenda of ordering society around the normative beliefs of the powerful, the elite, and the patriarchal authorities of the church (see Moreland 2001). Nevertheless, it is possible to explore how both individuals and communities used the architecture and materiality of early medieval crannogs to control and negotiate social relationships within their worlds. In particular, it seems that people used their liminality,

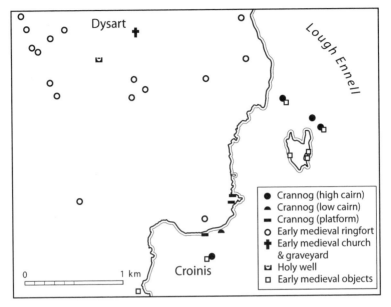

5. Map of the early medieval crannog of Cro-Inis, Lough Ennell, Ireland. A wider perspective reveals that the crannog island was set within a landscape of royal performance.

bounded nature and enigmatically distant architecture in discourses of power.

This is a motif that occurs in several early medieval texts. In the eighth-century *Life* of Aed mac Bricc, the saint waits impatiently at the harbour of the island of the king of Uí Néill on Lough Lene, Co. Westmeath, never to receive his invitation onto the island. Similarly, in the twelfth-century *Life* of Colmáin maic Luacháin, the saint goes to *Port na Inse* ('the harbour of the island'), and looks out at the king of Fir Tulach who was resident on his island of Inis na Cairrge, on Lough Ennell, Co. Westmeath. This motif of the saint or other personage standing on a lake shoreline awaiting impatiently the attention of the king out on his island is one that occurs in several of the saints' lives and also in the narrative literature. Incidentally, it

71

is also something we recently noticed ourselves, when investigating the early medieval crannog of Coolure Demesne, Lough Derravarragh. Our frequent local visitors, both the great and the good, often had to wait on the shoreline for some time. After standing there, listening with growing impatience to our inattentive chatter across the water, they would in the end call us on their mobile phones to send over a boat to pick them up. By contrast, early medieval kings who glibly ignored their shoreline visitors soon found themselves in trouble, as the saints caused the islands to sink miraculously beneath the water (O'Sullivan 2004).

A phenomenological and embodied perspective can be brought to bear on these ideas within actual archaeological landscapes. On the shores of Lough Ennell, Co. Westmeath, one of the most impressive of Irish early medieval royal crannogs, Cro-Inis, is situated about 80 m offshore. This was the royal site of the all-powerful Clann Cholmáin kings of the southern Uí Néill between the eighth and eleventh centuries AD. It is overlooked by another significant early medieval royal residence, the large raised ringfort of Dún na Sciath (the 'fort of the shields', also known as a royal site). Both places in this royal settlement landscape are physically and perhaps socially separated from the nearest 'ordinary' early medieval settlements (i.e. ringforts and churches) by 1.5 km of 'empty space'. It could be suggested that the crannog and ringfort, situated at the end of a long natural dryland peninsula flanked by fens and lake wetlands, are within a landscape of royal performance. A recent investigation of this space revealed that the modern visitor to the shore first walks across rich agricultural grasslands, possibly the royal *faitchi* or green, part of the king's estates, before the ringfort becomes visible on the skyline. Only upon approaching this site, does the crannog become visible, shimmering in the sun, distant, remote, and enigmatic (O'Sullivan 2004).

Thus early medieval crannogs may have been used in ideological ways to construct social identities of power and social class. Crannogs probably served as tribal strongholds, royal seats, summer lodges and as feasting places. However, the use of crannogs by kings may have been intentional in yet another way. Early medieval Irish kingship in the seventh and eighth centuries retained some pagan elements of earlier sacral kingship, albeit now within a Christianised context. The king was theoretically expected to symbolise the union of land and people, and thus retained some role as a mediator between the people and nature, between this world and the otherworld, which lay below the surface of a lake. The stories about kings on their crannogs, and the fact of their presence there, may have been intended to illustrate the king's role as a mediator with the forces of the watery otherworld, this being achieved by the location of his residence on a crannog. While the myths and stories conveyed this ideology orally, the physical location, form and appearance of the crannog signalled, on a day-to-day basis, the cosmological ordering or 'rightness' of the social structure. The ability to maintain such structures over the longer term would have contributed to the creation of myths and histories reinforcing the symbolic meaning of the crannog and the identities of its inhabitants.

It should also be pointed out that early medieval crannogs were occupied by lower social classes. Most early medieval crannogs would actually have been small islands situated in shallow water, close to their shorelines and accessed by stone or timber pathways or causeways. However, it is still the case that social groups were inhabiting wetlands, using water to construct a social distance and to bound the dwelling place. Recent survey and excavations on Lough Gara, Co. Sligo, reveal that many of the small crannogs there were occupied in the early medieval period, probably by ordinary farming groups, or occasionally by the landless, unfree or the poor. Fredengren (2002) argues that Lough Gara's crannogs were situated in places that were peripheral to the main settlement landscape of early medieval ringforts, churches, ogham stones and other 'tribal nodes'.

The early medieval crannog at Sroove, dated to between the seventh and tenth centuries AD, was used in diverse ways over time. It was initially a small island dwelling with a house enclosed within a wooden palisade. Its inhabitants left few material possessions, although they certainly had access to cattle, pig and sheep meat, as well as cereal grain. There was almost no attempt to 'exploit' the lake's wetland resources of fish, waterfowl or plant foods. The island was used towards the end of the early Middle Ages as an open-air iron-working platform, seemingly not as a settlement. Fredengren suggests that this shows how crannogs changed in meaning across time, using the idea of 'interpretative drift' to explore how people would have used this small site first as a domestic structure, then as an open-air platform of shattered stone used for forging iron, before it was abandoned. Interestingly, an early medieval crannog at Bofeenaun, Co. Mayo, was also used as an iron-working platform, with no evidence for houses, domestic debris or artefacts and abundant evidence for iron-slag, stone mortars and industrial activity (Keane 1995). We would suggest that crannogs like these should be interpreted as the island work-shops of blacksmiths, seen as semi-mythical personages in early medieval mythology on the edge of society, who used the boundaries of islands, water and distance to protect the arcane secrets of their trade, and were places of change. This would certainly fit with those modern ethnographic studies that suggest that smiths are often people who work at the edges of society.

Is it not paradoxical that islands could be places for kings at the same time as they could accommodate seemingly socially marginal(ised) groups, such as blacksmiths, the poor, women, the young and even monsters? However, liminality is a fluid and mutable concept and people could be both seeking and avoiding it, according to their social status, gender and role in the community. In the early Middle Ages, the king placed his royal residence on an island to achieve a social distance and a reputation for power, but at the same time he was at the physical and symbolic centre of the early medieval social landscape. The lord built his residence on a crannog to emulate the powerful, and to protect his own wealth and that of the community. The poor and socially marginalised may have been doing effectively the same thing – inhabiting places at the edge of land, maintaining their own identity and sense of place, while perhaps also being marginalised by others. Early medieval crannogs on lakes were places at the edge, at the same time as they were places at the centre of people's lives.

Incidentally, these observations echo early medieval developments in Holland in the ninth century AD (see Chapter 2), where socio-political developments transformed the wetlands from marginality into desirable places to live and work. We can assume that social identities were developed from this reclamation that stressed the rebellious and freedom-loving nature of these wetland dwellers. A water-based identity has since been actively invoked in periods of oppression with the term *Watergeuzen*, originally given to the maritime-based resistance to the Spanish in the Dutch War of Independence, and invoked again during subsequent periods of war. Of course, water and wetlands were utilised in the defence of the realm, and the Dutch *Waterlinie*, a line of moated forts on the edge of the lowlands of Holland, was maintained well into the twentieth century.

The drainage of the Humber Wetlands: rebels, resistance and contested waterlogged landscapes in the seventeenth century

In recent years many advances have been made in the understanding of the historic transformation of coastal wetlands, particularly in north-west Europe, and particularly through the work of our colleague Stephen Rippon in Wales and England.

75

Most interpretations of the reclamation of estuarine wetlands have emphasised changing economies, but it also possible to think about distinctive community identities. During the English Civil War, the Commoners of the Isle of Axholme in the Humber Wetlands, England, attacked and burned the settlement of Dutch drainage engineers at nearby Sandtoft (Cory 1985). This attack came about after many years of mounting anger and frustration, and the realisation by the Commoners that the promised benefits of the drainage of Hatfield Chase were not forthcoming. It also provides an intriguing example of the different perceptions of insiders and outsiders on the value of these wetlands, and how social identities can become polarised.

The myriad resources of the wetlands of Hatfield Chase, as these were available to the people of the Isle of Axholme, have been well documented. The higher, free-draining islands were used as arable land, typically farmed in the townfield system, with open strip fields surrounding nucleated settlements. Palaeoenvironmental research on Thorne and Hatfield Moors by Smith (1985), has shown an increased clearance of shrub and woodland, and intensification of agricultural activity after *c.* AD 1100. Crops included various cereals and hemp, used in the production of ropes which were much in demand by the navy. The minerogenic floodplains, comprising the riverside meadows and ings, were some of the most valued lands farmed as common lands within the townfield system. Used for grazing stock and as hay land, the meadows and ings provided the main source of food for livestock and plough animals. The lowest terrestrial areas, the carrs, moors and wastes, were extensively exploited as seasonal pastures and as such formed an essential part of the rural economy, enabling the use of some of the higher ings as hay lands. Furthermore, historical sources show that peat cutting, for fuel and as building materials ('turves'), was an important activity by the thirteenth and fourteenth centuries. One of the most surprising resources harvested from these low-lying areas in the Humber Wetlands were the wooden trees dug from the peat at Hatfield Moors and sold as ships' masts (Stovin Ms). The wet parts of the landscape were also valuable for seasonal grazing throughout the Middle Ages and the post-medieval period, for providing reeds for building, thatching and basket making, but even more importantly for fishing and fowling. Despite being highly regarded by the Commoners, from the perspective of the typically distant landowners, including the church and the crown, such a self-subsistence economy was a waste of ownership providing few, if any, taxes and revenues. Thus Hatfield Chase was described in a survey of 1608 as 'utterly wasted'.

Of course, the wetlands of the Humber basin were not the only such lands that were perceived favourably by the inhabitants but less favourably by their distant owners. In 1600 Parliament passed the *Act for the recovery and inning of drowned and surrounded grounds and the draining dry of watery marshes, fens, bogs, moors and other grounds of like nature*, intended for the extensive wetlands of the East Anglian Fenlands. However, it was first used in the Humberhead Levels, where the Dutch drainage engineer Cornelius Vermuyden was to undertake large-scale works that included the recutting of three rivers, the Don, Idle and Torne. The contract was signed with Charles I, but the Commoners were included in the considerations, and the newly drained lands were to be divided in equal parts between the king, Cornelius Vermuyden and his Participants (i.e. financiers), and the Commoners.

In many respects, however, the drainage was not the success hoped for by all, and the Commoners of the Isle of Axholme in particular complained bitterly. They noticed a reduced yield from fishing, the poor drainage of lands allocated to them and flooding of areas that had not been seasonally flooded before the drainage works started. This lack of achievement, on top of the

77

very different perceptions of the wetlands that existed between the insiders and outsiders before the drainage works commenced, expressed itself as opposing social identities during the English Civil War. The Participants and Commoners chose opposite sides, the former siding with the Royalists, the latter with the Republicans. This preference of the Commoners for the anti-royalist side in the conflict was not predicated in socio-political terms, but represents a choice that expressed their social identity. As part of their reformed social identities, the Commoners sabotaged much of the smaller drainage works, culminating in their attack on the drainage engineers' village at Sandtoft (Van de Noort 2004b).

Working in wetland landscapes and social identities

In the past, as today, daily life and practice would have been bound up with social roles or conventions, in terms of the types of labour done by different social classes, or the particular domestic tasks associated with men or women or children. These constrained their actions to some extent (e.g. a lord was unlikely to have done demeaning physical labour on a medieval fishtrap; an unfree person was unlikely to have worn ornate clothing and jewellery on a crannog). Inspired by Anthony Gidden's theory of structuration, archaeologists have explored how people may have been given some structured identities and roles upon birth, or through socialisation and upbringing (e.g. in the ways that a child would learn about the ways of the social world). Moreover, individuals and social groups often had *multiple* social identities, fluid and interwoven. So we need to think about how identities were fluid, mutable, and changing across a person's life.

On the other hand, it is also thought that people as agents could have defined and created these 'rules' themselves by behaving in regular and predictable ways, and that they could subtly alter and negotiate (to some extent) their social identities. In other words, people also had agency, an ability to make their own way, to choose and experience many different aspects of social identity, which could be manipulated when opportunity presented itself, or in different situations (albeit within social, ideological and physical limitations imposed by the social group). Thus people define and order their identities by their social relationships with each other. Identity is the dynamic interaction between individual and social group.

In these terms, social identity is never innate, it is about practice and is always 'in process'. Indeed, Giles (2001) has recently argued that archaeology has the unique ability to apprehend the material expression of such social identities through 'archaeologies of practice'. Wells (2001) has also argued that we can look at daily practices, tasks and routines that created a collective sense of identity and belonging. Similarly, Harris (2000) in a recent anthropological study of a Brazilian peasant village in the wetlands of the River Amazon, also suggests that this is a useful way of exploring identity. He stresses the importance of exploring what people do in their daily lives, their relationships with each other and the environments in which they live. We find such an approach attractive as wetland archaeologists because it looks at identity not within the politics and intellectual games of post-modernism, but because it is located in people's life and work and emphasises the practical, lived experience, and knowledge and engagement with the physical world, while it also allows us to contextualise this within people's historical and cultural experience.

Medieval fishing communities and the construction of collective identities

This is certainly an approach that can be usefully adopted when looking at the early medieval archaeology of estuaries in Britain and Ireland. Past studies have failed to take account of how people's ideas and beliefs about their landscapes would have been shaped by the ways in which they were used and moved around in everyday life. Surprisingly, there have been relatively few attempts to think about the ways in which people would have experienced and perceived these dynamic estuarine landscapes, or to recognise that wetlands were more than a source of economic benefit, but were also places where people constructed social identities.

Medieval fishtraps, for example, requiring constant maintenance and repair, were usually worked by small-scale operators, typically people who lived locally and who may have combined this activity with farming or other work. As a valuable source of income and revenue, fishtraps usually attracted attention from social elites (lords, bishops and monastic communities), and no doubt access to them would have been controlled and managed. However, we suggest that local fishing communities, through their practical knowledge and engagement with estuarine landscapes, actively constituted and negotiated their social identities through their daily work and seasonal practices.

Occasionally they used such knowledge and routines to effect a separation between themselves and others, to place themselves apart within the broader community. For example, one of the most striking aspects of estuarine archaeology is the quality of survival, and wooden structures that are often literally hundreds or thousands of years old can be available for inspection on every tide. It is worth remembering that people in the past, with their intimate knowledge of place, and of local folklore, may have recognised that these structures were relics of the past, and that they too would have used such 'archaeological knowledge' to construct and negotiate social and economic relationships within the communities in which they lived.

3. People of the wetlands?

6. A modern fishtrap in use on the Severn Estuary, Wales. Medieval fishing communities worked with evolving traditions and may have used their knowledge of the 'archaeology' of the mudflats to recreate distinctive social identities (photo: Chris Salisbury).

Fish was of course of social, economic and symbolic importance in the Middle Ages, with people's diet influenced by religious rules as well as customary practice. Recent intertidal archaeological surveys around Britain and Ireland have identified a wide range of medieval fishtraps used to catch fish, varying in location, style, size and details of construction. These also show interesting regional patterns, indicating that particular types evolved across time in different places to cope with variable dynamic estuarine environments (e.g. foreshores, currents, tidal ranges). However, it is also evident that the distinctively different types of fishtraps, and more importantly their long-lived continuities across time, were also the result of distinctive cultural practices of regional and local communities (O'Sullivan 2003b, 2003c, 2005).

Experiencing and understanding place and time in wetland landscapes

In estuarine landscapes, we can move beyond notions of identity that are defined in ethnic or class terms, and think instead about how people's daily encounters with the hidden and intimate places of the estuary – the narrow creeks winding their way through the reeds, the windswept islands out on the mudflats – would have influenced how they thought about themselves and others. Indeed, we can consider local communities as being partly defined by their work. This includes the local farming communities who moved their cattle, sheep and horses back and forth across the estuary marshes and islands. Local fishermen working every day out on the estuary's creeks and channels would have experienced a sense of separateness from the broader social community. These fishermen would have actively used their exclusive and specialist knowledge of these hidden places to create and sustain their own unique place within that community.

For example, people living and working in this landscape worked to different temporal rhythms. On an estuary, time is measured by a different clock; the moon rather than the sun determines the unique rhythms of the tides, the daily, monthly and seasonal cycles of low and high tides, of neap and spring tides. Indeed, people would themselves have marked time by the seasonal migratory movements of waders, ducks and geese. They would have watched for the seasonal movements of fish, the summer arrival of salmon, the autumn departure of eels. They would have observed the seasonal changes in vegetation, cutting reeds for thatch and basketry in early summer. If we think about how local fishing communities would have fished every low tide, including those night-time tides that are only lit by the moon, then we can get another sense of how they would have seen themselves as a distinctive social group.

3. People of the wetlands?

Anglo-Norman settlers, Gaelic Irish labourers and the construction of social identities amongst fishing communities

The earliest fishtrap structures on the Shannon estuary in south-west Ireland date to the fifth century AD, but the most intensive period of foreshore fishing activity seems to have been between the eleventh and the fourteenth centuries AD (O'Sullivan 2001a, 2001b, 2001c, 2004). The medieval fishtraps of these periods are quite similar in location, size and appearance. They are usually relatively small, being located in narrow mudflat creeks, where a single barrier could have literally sieved the water of all fish moving around with the tides. The fishtraps are designed to fish either the flooding or the ebbing tide, and in season people could have taken large catches of salmon, sea-trout, lampreys, shad, flounder and eels, the latter in October-November. An interesting feature of the Shannon estuary fishtraps is the strong continuity in their location and appearance through the late Middle Ages. We can see this most clearly in the medieval fishtraps beside the Anglo-Norman borough of Bunratty, on the north shore of the upper Shannon estuary. In the twelfth and thirteenth centuries, the Shannon estuary region was to witness significant political and ethnic changes. After the Anglo-Norman invasion of AD 1169, the local native Gaelic Irish lords, such as the O'Briens and the MacNamaras, were displaced by incoming colonisers and settlers, who first gained control of Limerick and then pushed westwards into the Gaelic lordships of the region.

In 1248 an Anglo-Norman manor was established at Bunratty, at a strategic location on the north bank of the estuary. In 1287 historical sources indicate that the borough of Bunratty had a castle, parish church, weekly market, annual fair, rabbit warren, water-mill and fishpond. It also had a sizeable population, with the presence of 226 burgages, implying a potential total of 1,000 people resident within the borough. Many of these townspeople would have been 'English' peasant farmers, tenants and merchants, settled on the new Anglo-Norman manors. While the Gaelic Irish social elites had been displaced, this does not suggest that all people of native Gaelic Irish ethnic extraction had departed. In fact, the archaeology of the medieval fishtraps suggests strong continuities in work and practice on the estuary mudflats below the borough. We can see this in the way that the same fishtrap types, identical in size, lay-out and construction were in use throughout the period of socio-political change.

A medieval fishtrap at Bunratty 4 (radiocarbon dated to AD 1018-1159) was a small V-shaped structure of post-and-wattle with a horizontal basket supported within a framework measuring 4.6 x 0.8 m. There is evidence that it was rebuilt and repaired on at least three occasions, suggesting that it had been used over decades. It was clearly built and used well before the Anglo-Norman colony was established, indicating Gaelic Irish settlement somewhere in the vicinity. Intriguingly, precisely the same style of fishtrap can be seen elsewhere on these mudflats, but probably dated to within the general period of the Anglo-Norman colony. At Bunratty 6, dated to AD 1164-1269, a fishtrap with a similar post-and-wattle fence, framework and well-preserved woven basket 4.5 m in length was probably placed on the bed of a mudflat creek, and would literally have taken every fish out of the water on the ebbing tide. Interestingly, then, the Bunratty fishtraps indicate that the same types of structure were in use before and after the Anglo-Norman colony. Similar patterns can be observed elsewhere on the Shannon estuary, and, indeed, elsewhere in England and Wales, before and after the Norman Conquest.

On the Shannon estuary we could explain this in terms of continuities of practice amongst local Gaelic Irish fishing communities. So, while the local Gaelic Irish lordship had been diminished by Anglo-Norman military power and economic investment, with upper social classes removed, we can imagine that the Gaelic Irish fishermen continued to work the channels in the manner of their forefathers. What we may be seeing here is the work of Gaelic Irish *betaghs* (from the Irish word *biatach*, meaning 'food provider') who are frequently mentioned in twelfth- and thirteenth-century historical documents. They seem to have lived in or near the Anglo-Norman manors, working as farmers, unfree tenants and labourers, ploughing land, harvesting crops and herding cattle. At Bunratty they may also have worked as fishermen, accommodating their work to the new social and political order. It could be argued that these were people who were deliberately working in ways that emphasised continuities with the past. In fact there are interesting parallels to be drawn with the First Nations fishing communities of the Pacific North West, who also see fishing as both a cultural and an economic resource within their communities, in the face of colonial intervention. The estuary, with all its dangers for the incomers who did not know their way in this treacherous environment, continued to be perceived as a unchanged place for those who had worked here for centuries.

Post-medieval fishtraps on the Shannon estuary:
a reinvention of tradition

We can take these ideas about landscape, practice and identity into the post-medieval period. In the eighteenth and nineteenth centuries, the economic resources of the Shannon estuary were also the focus of social and ethnic conflict. Limerick itself was a major Atlantic port at this time, with abundant historical evidence for ships and boats moving up and down the estuary on their way to ports in Britain, America and the West Indies. Fish, agricultural produce and timber were exported in return for salt, lead and iron. The estuary's marshlands were being reclaimed in a significant way, and were used for growing large crops of barley and oats. Labourers were employed to move cattle, sheep and horses across the saltmarshes and islands.

A historical and archaeological review of the Shannon estuary landscape reveals the extent to which it has always been a contested space, with lords, tenant farmers, labourers, mariners and fishermen all negotiating and competing for its resources. We can get an understanding of how these different social groups (i.e. English sailors, Irish sheep herders) were living and working on the estuary through the study of place-names, giving a sense of its 'alternative geographies'. On the Shannon estuary, various place-names provide information on topography and land-ownership. Tullyvarraga (*Tulach O'Bhearga* – O'Bhearga's hill), Clonmacken (*Cluain Maicin* – Macken's meadow) and Ballycasey (*Baile O'Cathasaigh* – Casey's place) are all of medieval Gaelic Irish origin, indicating mostly farming activities. On the estuary channel, there are a whole host of other names of rocks, islands and pools, mostly forgotten today, but preserved in nineteenth-century Admiralty Charts. These place-names – Battle Island, Dead Woman's Hand, Kippen Rock – are all of English origin, and testify to the fears and concerns of eighteenth- and nineteenth-century English-speaking mariners. There are also other estuarine place-names that were passed down through folk-tradition only, used to designate different stretches of the river to be used by net fishermen. Interestingly, these *enuires* (possibly deriving from the Middle English or Anglo-French term *en cure* meaning 'in use' or 'practice') on the river were not 'owned' by different families but by the entire fishing community, and were allocated to each member of the community in turn by agreement.

The Shannon estuary fisheries were an extremely valuable resource, and their ownership was a complex and tortuous subject. Fishing rights were jealously guarded and were often the subject of legal disputes over control and access, leading to unrest and even violence. By the nineteenth century, ownership of the larger fishtraps mostly resided in the hands of local landlords, bishops and the Limerick Corporation. The most obvious of these fishtraps are massive wooden ebb-weirs, with fences up to 250 m in length, located usually on the main estuary channel. Eighteenth- and nineteenth-century references refer to local poor people illegally building smaller structures to poach a resource which required no rent and which provided food and a supplemental income. Some of these can be identified as the smaller creek traps that are often located in hidden places, behind islands, or down in the creeks that dissect the deep muds. Both local landlords and net fishermen were loud in their criticisms of these fisheries, as they argued that fish-stocks were being destroyed and livelihoods being threatened. Ultimately, all these fisheries were to be banned by legislation in 1864, although, no doubt, people defiantly continued to use them in poaching activities.

Interestingly, on the Shannon estuary there were nearly always post-medieval fisheries close to or beside medieval examples. These are certainly not evidence for 'continuity', but they may not be accidental associations either. We believe that nineteenth-century fishing communities would have experienced deep historical time, through the recognition of ancient wooden structures in the muds. Fishing communities would have been experts on the materiality of the estuary. They would have recognised the peculiarity and unusual appearance of these medieval traps, with their small post-and-wattle fences and woven baskets on the mudflats. They might have recognised them as, in a sense, antiquities and used them as a source of information for good fishing places. This reminds us of the intimate knowledge that fishermen had of the creeks and channels, and how past material culture might have actively influenced their economic practices and social identities.

Conclusion

This chapter has explored how people who lived and worked in wetlands constructed and negotiated distinctive social identities within broader worlds. This forms a distinct departure from past approaches to the 'people of the wetlands', with their emphasis on de-socialised individuals, most notable in the form of bog bodies, whom we think we know so well, even intimately. This chapter has argued that people constructed social identities for themselves according to the places and times in which they lived, and according to the objects and animals with which they interacted, and that in the wetlands these constructions were often performed at the edges of society, on physical and environmental boundaries or at places that were often socially and ideologically liminal. The importance of the different perceptions of the wetlands held by insiders and outsiders as a key aspect in the creation, maintenance and alteration of social identities has been illustrated by case studies on crannogs in Ireland, wetland dwellers in England and the daily practice of fishing.

4

Lives and times in wetland archaeology: biographical approaches to material culture

Introduction

Wetland archaeologists, like other archaeologists, work with people, place and time. In earlier chapters we have discussed interpretative approaches to the perception and understanding of wetland landscapes, and ideas about communities, belonging and identity. We have already shown that amongst wetland archaeology's greatest strengths has been its ability to reveal the 'muck of life', the dirt underneath the fingernails of 'energetic commoners', the physical reality and materiality of peoples' existence. In this chapter we turn to the issue of time, and how wetland archaeology has contributed to our understanding of chronology, historical narratives and past people's perceptions of time.

First, we will discuss how wetland archaeologists might interpret time, from long-term continuity to short-term events in bogs, lakes and estuarine wetlands. Secondly, we will try to trace how people in the past themselves perceived and understood time. What did people think they were doing when they built sites, occupied and abandoned them? Thence, we also consider patterns of returning and renewal and will show how people reactivated places associated with the past for social and economic reasons.

Throughout, we suggest that wetland archaeologists need to

start thinking in more innovative ways about time, narratives and chronology, perhaps by using both anthropology and the cultural biographical approach to material culture that emphasises the shifting roles and meanings of a place or object over time and its cultural context. Recent studies of time by archaeologists have also failed to grasp the potential of wetland archaeology (e.g. Bradley 2002; Lucas 2005). We suggest that all archaeologists interested in the temporal rhythms of dwelling, the phenomena of remembering and forgetting, and cultural biographies of place and objects should look again at the astonishingly detailed narratives that it enables.

Dating the past in wetland archaeology

It is obvious that wetland archaeologists, like others, have long been interested in investigating, clarifying and interpreting the chronological aspects of material culture through typology, seriation, stratigraphy, and particularly scientific dating methods. Wetland archaeologists have had an advantage here, as their investigations have often revealed the organic and more readily datable evidence from settlements, including remains of houses, trackways, objects made of wood, leather and bone and environmental deposits, providing absolute rather than relative dates. Indeed, the use of incredibly fine-grained, precise site chronologies through dendrochronological analyses has been amongst the most striking of the contributions that wetland archaeology has made to the wider discipline. John Coles (2001, 31) has described how in wetland settlements each house may 'be assigned its real calendar date, to the year and perhaps to the season of the year' in which it was built.

There is something about such absolute dating that fires the imagination, belying Albert Einstein's famous dictum that 'the process of scientific discovery is a continuous flight from wonder'. In fact, it is difficult not to be inspired by a sense of wonder by wooden planks that have been dendrochronologically dated to a precise year (or season), whether that be 3806 BC (Sweet Track), 148 BC (Corlea 1 trackway) or AD 594 (Buiston crannog). Wetland archaeologists can also witness even more instantaneous moments in time. They can examine sharpened wooden posts with toolmarks that indicate a sequence of blows, some of them clumsy and poorly aimed. This is literally evidence for a precise instant in time, a vanished, distant moment that occurred thousands of years ago, when a long-dead person mishandled his axe through tiredness, inexperience or just by accident. Our sense of wonder derives from that personal connection with that other human being and our awareness that time has, for once, not annihilated a fragile, simple object.

Moving from the emotion of the moment to the whole story, wetland archaeologists have been able to use dendrochronology to write detailed narratives of origins, occupations and abandonments. For example, in the prehistoric lake villages of the Alpine foreland, dendrochronological dating has enabled an understanding to be gained about which houses were built first, when they were repaired, when other houses appeared and ultimately how settlement activities drifted back and forth across the site. Such a precise chronology has also revealed that many seemingly long-lived settlements had surprisingly interrupted lives, often being empty within fifty years of their first occupation. Similar dynamic pictures can also be seen at a landscape scale, for example as Neolithic and Bronze Age lake villages were constructed, abandoned and reoccupied over a period of only a few generations along a particular lakeshore. So wetland archaeology has the capacity to capture astonishing chronological evidence, but can it also offer explanations of wider relevance?

**People through time: interpreting 'continuity' and
'persistence' in wetland landscapes**

*From prehistoric trackways to early medieval
pilgrims' trails in Irish bogs*

Tracing long-term patterns of continuity and past people's
understanding of their own history has long been a subject of
interest in landscape archaeology (Bradley 2002; Lucas 2005).
Inspired by *Annales* scholarship, landscape archaeologists have
occasionally explored this continuity in terms of the *longue
durée*, a concept describing the environmental structures that
underpin long-term human use of the landscape (Bintcliff 1991;
Gosden 1994; Barrett 1989). Wetland archaeologists have
occasionally also thought about their landscapes in terms of
timelessness, persistence and endurance (e.g. Hall & J. Coles
1994; O'Sullivan 2001, 267-70). For example, John Coles and
David Hall (1998, 85) writing about the people of the Fenlands
of south-east England, refer to the 'stubbornness of the Fenlan-
ders – resistant to change, adhering to the way of life that had
its beginnings many centuries ago'.

Occasionally, wetland archaeology's ability to date sites
precisely through radiocarbon dating and dendrochronology (in
contrast to many types of archaeological sites whose chronology
may be more opaque) has enabled the discovery of interesting
patterns of continuity. In the Irish Midlands bogs, archaeological survey has enabled interesting new perspectives on the
motives behind early medieval monasticism. For example, the
early medieval monastic site of Lemonaghan, Co. Offaly was
established in the sixth century AD on a bog island, apparently
remote from other contemporary secular settlements (Stout
1997). The traditional interpretation of this 'monastic island'
would have been that it was the result of ascetic monks seeking
spiritual isolation in the wilderness, inspired by the writings of
the desert fathers such as St Anthony. However, archaeological

surveys in the raised bogs around the island revealed that there were numerous trackways there. Moreover, although some were contemporary with the early medieval monastery, radiocarbon and dendrochronological dating revealed that some of the trackways leading to and from the island were dated to the Bronze Age, Iron Age, early medieval and late medieval periods (McDermott 1998; O'Carroll 2001; Stanley 2003). So, far from being remote, Lemonaghan island should be interpreted as a place that was situated on a routeway that had been used, at least intermittently, since late prehistory. This would support the argument that instead of being placed in a remote location, the early medieval monastery had been cannily placed to serve as a hostel for travellers moving through the Midlands bogs, where it became a focus of pilgrimage.

Neolithic and Bronze Age trackways through time in the Somerset Levels

Wetland archaeologists have also been able to show that records of seeming continuity can mask interesting patterns of disruption and change. John and Bryony Coles (1992) reviewed the radiocarbon dating evidence for all the Neolithic and Bronze Age wooden trackways in the Somerset Levels that had been revealed by archaeological survey. Mapped in traditional terms, as 'Neolithic wetland landscapes' or 'Bronze Age wetland landscapes' with tens or hundreds of 'dots' on each map, the evidence would seemingly indicate long-term, continuous travel out from the drylands into the wetlands, to its islands or across to the other side.

However, the higher resolution analysis of the radiocarbon dates on a century-by-century basis indicated that in each hundred-year period there may have been only one or two trackways. In other words, the visible archaeological evidence indicates that instead of continuous activity and stability, there were merely years and at most decades of trackway use over several centuries in the wetlands. This is something that would be difficult, if not impossible, to achieve with Neolithic or Bronze Age lithic scatters on a dryland landscape. Indeed, it might be argued that in the study of the latter, archaeologists have tended to overemphasise the role of the *longue dureé*, not really realising that several Neolithic lithic scatters do not necessarily imply a long-lived, densely settled landscape. Indeed, if we want to understand the long-term occupation of a landscape, the wetland archaeological evidence is still superior as it demonstrates both aspects of persistence and distinctive temporal rhythms within it.

Interpreting the time-geography of Neolithic and Bronze Age lake dwellings

*Neolithic and Bronze Age lake villages:
settlement, economy and seasonality*

Perhaps wetland archaeology's most striking contribution to our understanding of time has come from the European Neolithic and Bronze Age lake settlements of the Alpine regions of Germany, France, Switzerland and Italy (e.g. Menotti 2004; Petrequin & Bailly 2004; Ruoff 2004). Neolithic lake villages have been excavated at many sites, particularly at various locations around Lake Constance and the Federsee in south-west Germany (Schlichterle 1997, 2004), and at Hauterives-Champreveyres on Lake Neuchatel (Egloff 1987, 1988) and at Sutz-Lattrigen on Lake Biel in Switzerland (Hafner 2004). In the French Jura there have been investigations of Neolithic lake dwellings at Clairvaux-les-Lacs and Chalain lakes (Pétrequin 1989, 1997; Pétrequin & Bailly 2004) and at Charavines-Les Baigneurs (Bocquet 1987; Bocquet & Huot 1994). After an apparent chronological gap in lakeshore inhabitation in the Middle Bronze Age (Menotti 2001), there are also numerous Late

Bronze Age lake villages around the region (Harding 2000), such as at Cortaillod-Est on Lake Neuchatel, Switzerland (Arnold 1986a, 1986b, 1990).

In the early Neolithic (4000-3300 BC), almost all settlement sites in the Alpine region were deliberately located on lake-shores or in their fens (Whittle 1996, 215-22). These were essentially hamlets or villages of rectangular wooden houses, with plank-floors, post-and-wattle walls and pitched, thatched roofs. Excavations have produced tremendously rich evidence for site organisation, habitation activities and material culture. The economy of these sites was based on the exploitation of both cultivated and foraged wild resources. Cattle were raised for meat and slaughtered young. Pigs, sheep and goats became more important as food sources over the period. However, much meat was provided by venison from the hunting of red deer, which also provided antler, a significant raw material for crafts (Schibler 2004). People also cultivated wheat, barley, flax and opium poppy, and bread has been found on some sites. The importance of wild resources can also be seen from the fact that textiles found on archaeological sites were usually made from plant fibres, not from wool. Palaeoenvironmental studies do not suggest large-scale woodland clearance, but cycles of short-lived activity. Indeed pollen and macrofossil studies of animal dung through the Neolithic also indicate that livestock grazed in small woodland clearances (Jacomet 2004).

Despite this broad-spectrum economy, these were village dwellers, not mobile, peripatetic farmers as has been suggested for other regions in Europe. In fact, the environmental evidence suggests that these lake-shore villages were full-time residences. Animal and bird bone analyses indicates the hunting and trapping of species that would have been available all year round. The presence of leaf fodder (elm, ash, lime) indicates that cattle were winter foddered on coppiced branches and leaves, while the surviving *pupae* of overwintering flies also suggest occupation during the winter, even when seasonal flood levels would have been high.

Dendrochronological evidence for village building, occupation and abandonment

Some of the most remarkable evidence to come out of the lake-village research of the last few decades is the recognition through scientific dating that these Neolithic lake-villages were occupied in very dynamic ways. Instead of being static, stable collections of many houses occupied across long periods, both absolute and relative dendrochronological dating programmes have indicated that the settlements often evolved rapidly from a few homesteads to larger villages, or alternatively down-shifted to smaller sites. It has also been possible to show that as some houses were being abandoned, others were constructed, so that occupation zones within a village shifted, tacked and changed across time.

At the German Neolithic lake dwelling of Hornstaad-Hörnle, for example, it has been possible to show that instead of a large settlement, it was a relatively small site that evolved and changed over about 90 years, between 3590 and 3500 BC (J. Coles 2001). Similarly, at the French Neolithic site at Charavines (occupied about 2740 BC), there were several phases of activity over a 60-70 year period (Bocquet & Huot 1997, 21-8). In its earliest years, the dwelling comprised no more than two to three buildings situated between the forest and the lake. Ten to fifteen years later, it had become a more substantial settlement with at least five large buildings and an enclosing palisade. However, by the eighteenth to twentieth year of activity, many of these buildings had been abandoned. It was only after thirty to forty years that people returned and rebuilt a second village on the ruins of the old one.

John Coles (2001) describes another well-known example in

4. Lives and times in wetland archaeology

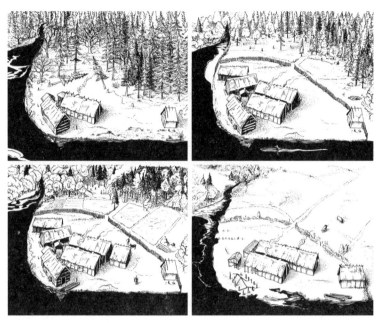

7. Reconstruction drawings illustrating how dendrochronology revealed the dynamic sequence of site construction, occupation and contraction of a Neolithic lake village at Charavines, Lac de Paladru, France (based on Bocquet and Houot 1994: 21-4). Top left: years 1 and 2; top right: years 3 to 8; bottom left: years 9 to 17; bottom right: years 18 to 22.

the Hautcrives-Champreveyres site – a Neolithic lake-village on the north bank of Lake Neuchatel, in western Switzerland. The site produced thousands of posts, and although patterns of rectilinear structures and a possible enclosing palisade could be discerned, it was impossible by standard archaeological analyses to establish a sequence to the structures. However, species identifications and dendrochronological analyses made it possible to trace the evolution of the site. At 3810 BC, a rectangular house was built on the site, to be followed by two houses to the east and three to the west. At 3804 BC, a small building was constructed. In 3801 BC, a large rectangular building was placed to the west, at the same time as small square buildings and a fence were placed on the foreshore. In the next year, 3800 BC, two small structures were built on the site. Over the following seven years, between 3800 and 3793 BC, small repairs were carried out around the site. Sometime after 3790 BC the site was probably abandoned. So although Hauterives-Champreveyres was at times a relatively large settlement of six houses, it evolved slowly across time and was abandoned within seventeen years of its first occupation.

Similar patterns can be seen on Late Bronze Age lake village sites around the Alpine region, such as at Cortaillod-Est, on Lake Neuchatel, Switzerland (Arnold 1986a, 1986b, 1990). Houses and buildings on this site were built and repaired very fast, within two to three years. Tree-ring studies indicate that the quality of timber used deteriorates through the phases of construction, suggesting exhaustion of suitable timber resources within a 1 km radius. Cortaillod-Est was occupied for only fifty years. Hafner (2004, 186-7) has recently described the Late Bronze Age village of Böschen, on the Greifensee in Switzerland, which was probably built in 1047-1046 BC. It comprised up to twelve substantial rectangular domestic buildings enclosed on the watery side by a substantial palisade, while towards the shore there may also have been smaller storage buildings and a protective fence. This site was probably also abandoned within a decade, but in this case probably following a catastrophic fire.

The abandonment of sites and landscapes within regions

Wetland archaeologists have also been able to reconstruct dynamic settlement histories of landscapes, regions and localities. On Lake Constance in south-west Germany, an unsophisticated archaeological mapping of Neolithic lake villages would seemingly show a fairly densely settled landscape of five contemporary Neolithic lake dwellings along a ten-kilometre stretch of the eastern shore. However, as Bryony Coles (1999)

4. Lives and times in wetland archaeology

showed in her analysis of the dendrochronological dates, Neolithic communities were abandoning villages and moving on to other neighbouring places, sometimes returning after a period to the original site, sometimes going elsewhere.

At Hornstaad-Hornle IA, the earliest Neolithic village was built around 3912 BC. This was probably burnt down and immediately repaired in 3904 BC. The entire site was probably abandoned in 3900 BC. Immediately upon the abandonment of the Hornstaad-Hornle IA village, two other lake-villages appear further along the lakeshore, one at Hemmenhofen-im-Bohl constructed at 3900 BC, the other at Gaienhofen constructed at 3890+/–10 BC. After forty years, some people then clearly returned to Hornstaad-Hornle II to build a new village. Finally, the latest village in this local sequence is found at Wangen-Hinterhorn, constructed in 3825 BC. This then was potentially one Neolithic community, literally upping sticks and moving along the shore at intervals, rather than several communities living along the lakeshore at the same time (B. Coles 1999).

Equally as challenging to our notions of Neolithic settlement permanence is provided by the lakeshore villages recently investigated at Sutz-Lattrigen, on the Lake of Biel, Switzerland (Hafner 2004). Here there were as many as twenty Neolithic villages on a small part of the lake between 3840 BC and 2688 BC. The earlier Neolithic villages at Innere Hauptstation date to across the period, 3840-3566 BC. At a later stage, the Neolithic village of Reidstation had been built after an absence of activity for 170 years and was located only 200 metres from the earlier sites. Beginning in 3393 BC, nineteen buildings were erected over a period of five years. It was a village like the others, with rows of large rectangular buildings oriented at right angles to the shoreline. However, the site was abandoned after only six years, as the dendrochronological record ends at 3388 BC. Lake levels rose and there was an occupation hiatus of 180 years, to be followed by more village occupation (Hafner 2004, 189-91).

Interpreting chronological patterns of site abandonment and reoccupation

As John Coles (2001, 31) has stated, such patterns of periodic site abandonment and reoccupation raise serious questions about settlement mobility, environmental and woodland exhaustion and the social and political factors involved in such instability and movement. In any case, archaeologists have interpreted the cycles of this record in various ways, depending on the chronological and spatial scale of their analysis. Individual village abandonment is often interpreted in terms of micro-regional environmental change (e.g. flooding, destruction by fire), whereas in interpreting it as a phenomenon that occurred across central Europe over hundreds of years, archaeologists have tended to think in terms of environmental change and cultural and population displacement (Menotti 2001). Indeed, in contrast to most empirical wetland archaeological approaches, some of these studies have been explicitly theoretical, adopting the principles and approaches of cultural ecology and neo-Darwinian evolutionary theory (e.g. Shennan 2000; Menotti 1999, 2003, 2004).

Climate change has been seen as a significant factor. Sedimentary studies and analyses of radiocarbon atmospheric residual curves (an indirect indicator of atmospheric and climatic conditions) have been used to suggest that lake villages were often built at a time of climatic and environmental improvement across the Alpine regions, when lake shores may have been drier. Conversely, periods of climatic deterioration and increased rainfall may have lead to rising water levels, severe flooding and the abandonment of both lakeshore settlements (Magny 1993; Menotti 2001, 211; Pétrequin & Bailly 2004, Fig. 3.3). However, there were also optimum climatic periods at other times of prehistory (e.g. in the Early and Middle Bronze Age) when there is a long hiatus in the use of lake villages, suggesting that social and cultural reasons for the abandonment of lakeshore dwellings have to be considered. Menotti (2001, 2004) suggests that during the Middle Bronze Age former lake-dwelling communities shifted into the dry-lands, and through their contacts and acculturation with other groups, adapted their societies, economies, material culture and lifeways to suit drier environments and turned their back on the wetlands.

There is a range of material and palaeoenvironmental (i.e. pollen) evidence that prehistoric populations were not steady or constant during the Neolithic and Bronze Age. Archaeologists and palynologists have therefore suggested that population dynamics and human demographic change influenced the settlement and abandonment of lakeshores. For example, Petrequin and Bailly (2004, 45) argues that between 3200 and 3000 BC (a period of climatic upturn), the Clairvaux and Cha-lain lakes in the French Jura were colonised by two different migrant populations that used distinctive pottery and architec-tural styles. These peoples built an ever-increasing number of villages, and their population increase is indicated by the fact that they moved from the use of firstly young, secondary-growth trees before they attacked the more remote and ancient, primary wood-land oaks. Then, suddenly, between *c.* 2900 and 2700 BC these precisely dated Neolithic lake dwellings were abandoned (at a general period of climatic deterioration). Yet, there is no nearby dryland archaeological or pollen evidence to suggest that these people had moved upslope to a more favourable habitat. Moreover, there is also a decline in the number of other types of archaeologi-cal sites across the Jura and west Switzerland region, suggesting a regional population density decline or even collapse. The image of pandemic disease, not often invoked by archaeologists, might be raised here, although there may have been other reasons.

We suggest that there are other interesting social and ideo-logical factors to consider in interpreting the occupation and

101

abandonment of lake dwellings. Initially, many Neolithic lake villages may have been built for essentially social and political reasons, such as a concern for safety and defence by a migrant population or during a time of conflict for land and resources. However, anthropological studies indicate that settlement abandonment could have been a complex cultural process (Cameron & Tomka 2003). Ethnographic studies show that amongst small-scale communities, dwellings and villages are often understood to have life-cycles that mirror human lives. As people were born, lived, grew old and died, so also dwellings could be built and extended, deteriorate and collapse. In some societies, there is a strong symbolic association between the life of a dwelling (or village) and the life of the people (or community) that dwell within it. Therefore, at the death of a person who is most strongly associated with it (a tribal leader or shaman, say), there can be an act of abandonment, and the dwelling may even be burnt down. Indeed, the Late Bronze Age village of Böschen mentioned above could have been deliberately torched for some reason *during* its abandonment, rather than being abandoned *because* of an accidental fire.

On occasion, settlement abandonment can certainly be related to the over-exploitation of the local environment or a population collapse. However, communities also change organically. Within generations they expand and contract as children are born, as people move away or as the elderly die. It is surely interesting that many of the Neolithic lake villages described above change within periods that might be described as two generations (i.e. 50-60 years). In the normal way, communities also experience the contingencies of local events and incidents, so we should expect that each Neolithic or Bronze Age village had its own specific occupation history, related to events we will never know about. For example, ethnographic studies reveal that houses and dwellings can be abandoned for many reasons, for example an unusual or disturbing occurrence in the community, such as the 'bad death' (murder, unlucky or violent death, sudden sickness) of a significant member of a community (Brück 1999). Settlements might be abandoned as a result of a belief that a dangerous spiritual force or malady was present. Finally, it is worth bearing in mind that even when a village is abandoned as a settlement, it may continue to be used in less intensive ways (for example, as a garden, a place for storage or a corral for livestock). It may also be a place of memory – a place associated with ancestors or historical events – to be either avoided or returned to. Indeed, this might explain why sites like Hornstaad-Hornle II were actually reoccupied.

Tracing the cultural biographies of wetland sites and objects

Functionalist approaches to material culture in wetland archaeology

Wetland archaeologists have often explored in a general way the use-lives of broad classes of artefacts such as wooden track-ways, wooden bowls and tubs, bone pins and basketry (e.g. Bernick 1998; Croes 2001). Following on from this, when looking, for example, at wooden bowls, wetland archaeologists would reconstruct the management and procurement of the original raw materials (e.g. woodland management of ash poles), the felling and modification of timber, and the carving out of rough-outs and blanks, as well as analysing the various tools used.

These analyses would move on to consider the methods and techniques of the final manufacture and finishing of the object (carving or pole-lathe turning), its use across time (e.g. the unique evidence for staining by foodstuffs and the physical traces of wear and use). The growing age of the object might be traced through analysis of its re-use and repair (the use of repair patches and stitching, or even the hacking down of a

103

spoon to a small spatula); its deterioration and damage. A good example might be the broken wooden bowl from the Bronze Age lake dwelling at Fiavé, Italy, that had been repaired, indicating that the life of this cherished object was prolonged through skilled craftsmanship (Perini 1988a, 1988b).

Cultural biographical approaches to material culture in wetland archaeology

However, wetland archaeologists rarely explore the changing perceptions and meanings of a place or object across time. It might be useful then to look at wetland landscapes, sites and objects in terms of their cultural biographies (e.g. Appadurai 1986; Koptyoff 1986). The cultural biographical approach proposes that between the moment an object is produced to the moment it is discarded or forgotten, it goes through several culturally-specific phases. In each, its function, status and people's perception of it may change, and through use and handling by different people it acquires a history or a biography.

Recent approaches to material culture biographies consider many different aspects of the social and ideological meanings of objects through time, space and changing material circumstances. They attempt to reconstruct what objects meant to people across time, and indeed how they themselves shaped people's understandings and social relationships. For example, Kopytoff (1986, 67) briefly described the biographies of huts among the Suku people of Zaire. A hut initially shelters a couple or a mother and child. After some years, it may serve as a guest-house for visitors, or as a kitchen, and finally it descends to the role of a chicken coop, before it collapses. However, it is not possible for the biography to go in the other direction, as it would be socially unacceptable for a kitchen or chicken coop to be turned into a dwelling. Archaeological studies of Neolithic houses in south-east Europe (Tringham 1995), Middle Bronze

Age houses in southern Britain (Brück 1999) and Iron Age houses and farmsteads in the Netherlands (Gerritsen 1999) have suggested that prehistoric dwellings also had biographies and life-cycles practically and metaphorically linked to the lives of the people who used them.

Both dwellings and objects then have potentially complex biographies linked to a particular set of cultural ideas, as well as to the particularities of their social and material circumstances. It is interesting then that Gerritsen (2003, 38) states that wetland archaeological sites with their 'detailed evidence about successive phases of use, reconstruction and abandonment' produce the best evidence to support the writing of a 'truly detailed archaeological biography'.

A cultural biography of an Iron Age vessel from Toar Bog, Ireland

An Iron Age wooden trough from Toar Bog, Co. Westmeath, provides a brief example of the potential of these approaches. This vessel was recently recovered during archaeological surveys of this bog in the Irish Midlands (Murray 2000; Moore *et al.* 2003, 134). It was a large, carved tub or trough, rectilinear in shape (1.3 m long x 60 cm wide), with handles at the end and spectacularly well-preserved details that suggested that its role and function had shifted and changed across time.

The wooden vessel was clearly always intended to be something special. First, it was carved from an unusually thick and mature alder tree (54 years old) suggesting that it was intended to be impressively and uniquely large. It was carved using possibly five axes and at least one gouge, suggesting the work of several people. It actually split in the last few hours of its manufacture. Close to the handle a very fine crack started to develop from the heartwood, but its makers used four tiny, cleverly-spaced wooden wedges to staple this crack together.

105

8. Iron Age wooden trough found at Toar Bog, Co. Westmeath, Ireland. Archaeological excavation and analysis reveals aspects of the object's biography (photo: Irish Archaeological Wetland Unit).

This repair definitely occurred during manufacture, as subsequent carving deliberately reduced their appearance to near invisibility.

For a time the vessel was used for some high-status activity, perhaps feasting and the display of fine foods. The toolmarks on its outer surface are pristine, suggesting it was not moved around much or roughly handled. It is conceivable that the vessel was produced for some special event, perhaps a ritual meal associated with a marriage, a funeral ceremony or a significant rite of passage. For example, early Irish kings reputedly bathed in horses' blood upon their inauguration.

It was soon to shift in meaning. After a short time a second crack appeared along the edge of the vessel where its narrow sides reduced its strength, perhaps as the wood dried. This was also repaired using small carved wooden panels on the inner and outer surface, secured by slight wooden ties through perfo-

rations in the vessel's sides. But this crack somehow changed
the meaning of the object, perhaps spoiling it in some way. Now,
it was to be employed in a more domestic context, such as salting,
curing, tanning or dyeing. Fire-scorching along the top edge after
the second repair suggests it was perhaps used in cooking or the
heating of water for washing and bathing; small stone chips found
in the vessel might suggest hot-stone technology.

But the perception and social meaning of the vessel was to
change once more. At the end of its life, or somebody else's life,
the wooden trough was ritually killed. People used withies to
carry the heavy object out into the bog, where they placed it in
waterlogged, reedy conditions. Propped upright by long,
vertical pegs, it was also pinned down by a forked branch,
similar to a number of Iron Age bog bodies. Radiocarbon dating
indicates that the vessel was abandoned sometime between
about 197 BC and AD 68. There it settled, sinking into the mire,
awaiting its rediscovery and re-use by Irish archaeologists,
which is the latest stage in its biography.

*Building, occupying and abandoning an early medieval
crannog at Buiston, Ayrshire, Scotland*

Striking evidence for the cultural biographies of dwelling places
and the 'muck of life' has also been revealed by archaeological
excavations of an Iron Age and early medieval crannog at
Buiston, Ayrshire in south-west Scotland (Barber & Crone
1993; Crone 2000). Buiston crannog, during the main phase of
its occupation in the sixth to seventh century AD, was probably
the island stronghold of a small community of farmers, who were
fairly self-sufficient and prosperous without being particularly
wealthy.

Initially, radiocarbon dating seemed to indicate a long period
of occupation at Buiston, from the second to the seventh century
AD. Both the archaeological evidence and these radiocarbon

9. Reconstruction drawing of an early medieval crannog at Buiston, Ayrshire, Scotland. Dendrochronological studies indicated the surprisingly dynamic picture of the site's occupation and abandonment, confirming the ability of wetland archaeological sites to reveal site biographies (drawn by Alan Braby, reproduced with the permission of Historic Scotland, from Crone 2000).

dates, if found at all on a dryland site, would be taken to indicate a fairly long history of continuity, but things were a lot more interesting than that at Buiston crannog. Dendrochronology indicated that the site's history of occupation and abandonment was surprisingly dynamic and compressed into a relatively brief eighty-year period, between AD 589 and 630. In other words, the people of Buiston lived there for only two generations, during which time they were constantly struggling with the difficulties of their marshy, unstable living conditions. Periods of flooding were interspersed with sudden events when the palisades and houses collapsed, and people were constantly rebuilding and replacing structures.

To begin with, there was some activity on the site in the Late Bronze Age and some of these timbers were later to be used in the early medieval levelling of the crannog. In Phase I, the first to second century AD, a primary mound of stone, timber, brushwood and turves was built on the lakebed and occupied, before it was abandoned, grassed over and subsequently submerged. For the next three hundred years, the site lay silent and abandoned through Phase II, until some short-lived activity or palisade building at about AD 550, that may well have ended in fire.

For some reason, people returned to this place at the end of the sixth-century AD, at about AD 589 to build an island dwelling. This may have been the accidental re-use of shallows in the water or a piece of raised ground in the marshy vegetation. It may also have been the deliberate reactivation of an antique site which had associations with ancestors, a common phenomenon in both Ireland and Scotland (Crone 1993; Henderson 1998; O'Sullivan 1998; Fredegren 2003).

This Phase III crannog was built as a small 'packwerk' crannog. A mound of timber, brushwood and stone was dumped onto the earlier and natural lacustrine muds that had accumulated during the abandonment. On this were placed layers of peat and turves taken from local agricultural slopes. It was enclosed within a double palisade, which, again, re-used some planks from the *c.* AD 550 activity, and was rebuilt and resurfaced on a number of occasions. This phase produced evidence for at least one early medieval house (House A) represented only by an arc of posts from a roundhouse possibly 5.6 m in diameter. It was occupied for five years; within that period the hearth and floor were replaced three times.

Insect studies reveal large numbers of fly puparia, indicating that people would have endured great swarms of house-flies that thrived in the rotting organic material lying on the floor (also indicated by beetles who inhabit rotting vegetation). So plentiful were these flies that people might have suffered from maggots and fly-borne skin diseases. Do these studies indicate that living conditions in House A were sufficiently unpleasant to warrant its abandonment? Alternatively, do they indicate the intensity of life on the site during a hot summer, or indeed are there flies there *because* of site abandonment? A period of flooding ensued, but the people returned again.

In AD 594 the entire crannog was levelled and rebuilt, extending its surface further towards the north-west, suggesting a change in the household group. Some of this work may have been interrupted by a season's absence, as reeds grew *in situ*. House B, a roundhouse 8 m in diameter with internal partitions, and the largest house to be used on the dwelling, was constructed of a double wall of post-and-wattle. Perhaps the social status of the site's inhabitants had been transformed, enabling them to dwell within a larger structure. It could also mean that the household group itself had expanded, perhaps as grandparents moved in with a younger family. House B was used as a dwelling for the next twenty years, during which time the hearth and floor were replaced four times, every five years or so, the last time in AD 609.

In AD 620 the site's inhabitants decided to consolidate the site with something more substantial and a timber ringbeam palisade was constructed, perhaps with a walkway, to be followed by an arc of alder stakes in AD 630. At some stage this palisade collapsed out again. People continued to occupy the site, but now it was moving towards the final phases of its occupation and the crannog was probably abandoned by AD 650.

Palaeoecological studies of the waterlogged deposits have given various insights into the living conditions of the site's inhabitants. Insect studies revealed that there were relatively few beetles in the deposits, possibly reflecting the fact that the site did not see continuous occupation. Sheep parasites probably indicate the presence of sheep skins brought in for wall hangings and bedding. The absence of cattle dung indicates that animals were not kept on the site. However, the site belonged to a farming group who worked the local landscape. Cattle, sheep and pig and even geese were tended and eaten. Wooden churn lids demonstrate the importance of dairying and butter-making, and a wide range of cultivated foodstuffs, including barley, oats and linseed, were consumed. Quern stones attest to the preparation of some grain for porridge or bread making. Interestingly for an early medieval settlement, wild foods and red deer and roe deer were also hunted.

Perhaps the most fascinating aspect of Buiston crannog is the revelation of how people constantly struggled and coped with mucky, damp conditions, perpetual flood waters, structural collapse and buzzing flies. They chose to live with the problems of slumping and structural collapse, as waterlogged deposits settled into position and slid outwards. All of this evidence, difficult as it is to interpret and understand, would be lost on a dryland site. It also gives some sense of the fact that for one household or social group over two generations, this island dwelling was a place of constant work and renewal, with houses and palisades rebuilt, floors relaid and hearths reconstructed at very short intervals indeed.

Interpreting past people's perception and experience of seasonal rhythms

Anthropological and archaeological perspectives on seasonal change

We should also reflect on how people in the past may have perceived the passage of shorter periods of time. Anthropologists suggest that small-scale communities think about the past in quite diverse ways (Ingold 1993, 1995; Harris 2000; Lucas 2005,

111

62-4). Many do perceive the distant past in terms of history and ancestors. People also understand time in terms of cycles of seasonal rhythms. Occasionally this may be calendrical, involving the recognition of lunar cycles, changes in tides and the location of constellations in the sky. However, as Harris (2000, 126) states, people also monitor and 'attend to' seasonal changes in the environment; rains and wind, the rise and fall of riverine water levels, bird and fish migrations, the fertility and move-ment of animals, the cyclical growth and decay of plant life and so forth (Ingold 1993, 65; O'Sullivan 2005).

Wetland archaeologists have long been interested in season-ality and often explain their sites in terms of the perceived past use and exploitation of economic resources that vary from winter to summer (e.g. reeds, wood, birds, game, seasonal grazing, etc.). However, it is time to move beyond explanations that focus only on economic and subsistence activities and start to think about how past people's social identities, relationships and beliefs were also connected to seasonal rhythms.

Harris's (2000) anthropological study of a community of *caboclo* fisherpeople who live in the village of Parú, on the banks of the River Amazon, Brazil, offers potentially interesting insights. He suggests that seasonality is intrinsic to the prac-tices and social relationships of the people who dwell within this riverine wetland landscape, and that these relationships have a distinctly rhythmic character that 'resonates' with changes in the seasons (Harris 1998; 2000, 125-41). Most importantly, these seasonal changes are the 'frame of life' within which people's *social lives* are performed. These ideas are in keeping with recent shifts in Amazonian anthropological theory that has moved on from western models of cultural ecology and subsistence economics to ideas that are more rooted in indigenous collective identities and an emphasis on 'conviviality' – the importance of living communally, and well, together (Overing & Passes 2000).

4. Lives and times in wetland archaeology

For the wetland dwelling people of Parú, there are distinct social and aesthetic differences between the 'wet season' and 'dry season'. During the wet season (between December and June), rising water in the river and its lakes submerges people's agricultural land, leaving them isolated within their houses. Fish are difficult to catch, and crops impossible to cultivate – so they live at home, doing odd jobs, sewing, mending, and teaching children. This is a time of inner family life, introversion, disconnection – people swing in their hammocks, watch the floodwaters listlessly through the floorboards or occasionally visit close neighbours by boat. People feel cold, their being-in-the-world makes them feel miserable and wretched, they complain about food shortage and that the flood destroys all their labours (Harris 1998, 2000).

By the beginning of the 'dry season' in June, the flood waters are retreating and the land appears, now covered in rich fertile mud. People's social lives explode; they wander around the village, work and chat together animatedly, making plans for the best months of the dry season. Men spend more time away from the house; hunt in the forest; fish from boats with nets; sleep in huts by the river and gather together spontaneously to work in a relaxed way on their gardens. Women also move out into the village, helping each other with work and children. Men and women gather for parties, they visit distant kin, and they build temporary huts without fireplaces by the lakeshores so they can remain close to good fishing grounds without the need to return to their villages. This is a 'beautiful time', a joyful time of plenty, eating, boisterous partying, as well as courting and sex in the forest for unmarried couples. In other words, people's wetland economic practices are contingent on their social and gender relations that themselves are dependent on seasonal and environmental changes (Harris 2000, 140-1).

113

*Building and returning to Iron Age marshland houses
at Goldcliff, Severn estuary, Wales*

It may be interesting to explore these ideas in the context of prehistoric dwellings in wetlands. Recent wetland archaeological projects on the estuaries of Britain and Ireland have uncovered much evidence for what seem to be Bronze Age and Iron Age houses, trackways and platforms in environmental contexts that were originally saltmarshes and fens. In general, it is thought that these were houses and structures used by people herding cattle and sheep on estuarine marshes during spring and summer. It should be pointed out that there are other Bronze Age structures and features, for example spreads of burnt stone, charcoal and animal bone, that are not so easily interpreted in economic terms, while the recovery of Bronze Age metalwork and skulls from some sites suggests that there may also have been ritual activities in these places between land and water (see O'Sullivan 2001, 128-33).

Amongst the most striking of these discoveries are the Iron Age houses investigated on intertidal peats at Goldcliff West, on the Welsh shore of the Severn estuary. These large rectangular structures were originally constructed on raised hummocks in a raised bog or on fen-peats at the edge of an estuary. Dendrochronological and radiocarbon dates suggest their construction and use in the fifth to early third centuries BC (Bell 1993a, 1993b, 1999; Bell *et al.* 2000). The buildings were quite substantial, measuring 5-8 x 4-6 m. The walls were constructed of alder roundwood and oak planking, entrances were situated at the ends, and internal or axial posts suggest that at least some of the structures were roofed. Where evidence survived, there were indications of flooring of rough roundwood, reeds or straw. Palaeoenvironmental analyses suggest that the Iron Age Goldcliff houses relate to medium-term periods of increased marine transgression, when marine flooding may

114

10. Reconstruction of Iron Age building 1 at Goldcliff, Severn Estuary, Wales. A range of archaeological, dendrochronological and palaeoenvironmental evidence revealed episodic use, perhaps as summer habitations for people herding cattle on the marshes. Anthropological evidence also suggests that both social and economic activities resonate with seasonal rhythms (drawn by Steve Allen, from Bell *et al.* 2000).

have altered local vegetation in ways that made the raised bogs good places for grazing animals.

Remarkably, hundreds of cattle hoof prints were identified in the clays of the channels around the structures. These clearly indicate the congregation of animals around the structures and one is reminded of the tendency of cattle today to stand in pools of water on hot summer days, literally cooling their heels. Beetle studies at Goldcliff indicated the presence of decaying vegetation, animal dung and reeds around the houses. Lice in the palaeochannels also indicated the presence of cattle and the identification of human fleas suggested that both people and cattle were living inside these structures (Bell 1999; Bell & Neumann 1996, 1997, 1998). This scenario is similar to that found at Site Q, in the Assendelver Polders of The Netherlands, where Iron Age rectangular buildings with internal divisions have been interpreted as dwelling places for both people and cattle (Therkorn *et al.* 1984). Only a few finds were recovered from the entrances or in the palaeochannels around the Goldcliff buildings, including wooden withy ties and bucket fragments. These are objects that might be interpreted as being associated with milking and hobbling cattle.

Bell (1999) suggests that there may have been episodic activity at the Goldcliff houses 'extending over periods of years'. Dendrochronological evidence suggests that Goldcliff Buildings 1 and 2 were rebuilt over multiple phases of activity over some time, perhaps up to seventeen years. Goldcliff 6 probably had a shorter life. Beetle analyses and the identification of lenses of clay between occupation horizons also suggest episodic use, interspersed by periods of flooding under brackish water. The lack of hearths, charcoal and ash within the Goldcliff houses suggest that these were seasonally occupied sites and not domestic habitations in the conventional sense. Bell (1999, 23) concludes from the presence of neonatal calf bone (calves are typically born in the spring months) that occupation was between May and June, when tides were lowest and the bogs would not have been so regularly inundated by the monthly high spring tides. There are also Iron Age trackways in the Goldcliff peats that run for up to a hundred metres and directly approach these buildings, either from the estuary channel or bedrock islands in the levels. Intriguingly, these trackways were made of wood cut in the winter and might have been constructed in the winter to enable activities in the marshes, such as trapping ducks and geese (Bell 2003, 13).

It is possible that the people using these buildings lived in the substantial Iron Age hillforts that dominate the Gwent Levels from the dryland to the north. It is also possible that they occupied smaller Iron Age enclosed and unenclosed settlements at the edge of the levels. However, the Goldcliff Iron Age buildings are 'odd' in several ways. For example, apart from their rectangular shape, their entrances are generally oriented north-west, whereas most Iron Age round house entrances face towards the rising sun. Bell (2003, 12) has usefully suggested that the rectangular character of the buildings and the lack of pottery, which contrasts with most Iron Age dryland settlements in England and Wales, might indicate that these were wetland communities with 'an impoverished material culture and distinctive identity from those occupying the surrounding hillforts and upland'.

However, instead of being the dwellings of a different people, it seems more likely that these Iron Age houses are architecturally distinctive because of *when* they were used; and that they are expressing notions of social identity, lifeways and time. They may be rectangular and have oddly-oriented entrances precisely because they are *summer dwellings,* thus representing in a material way the 'dry season' and all the other social and aesthetic experiences that came with it. This enables us to think again about the ways that people's identities were not merely constructed in collective, ethnic or class terms, but through what they did and the time of the year they did it. It is evident that people came out here in spring and summer, stayed for a while and left again and that they did this over a period of years. In anthropological studies of cattle trans-humance groups, each household or extended social group is responsible for the maintenance of its own hut at the summer grazing places. It is interesting then that at Goldcliff there are subtle architectural and technological differences between each building, suggesting that they too belonged to different social groups who repaired them every year.

How about the social and aesthetic aspects of these seasonal economic practices? Summer saltmarshes are pleasant places to be. We might imagine that people did enjoy the sunny months out on the marshes, freed from the winter *ennui* of dryland life in a dark, smoky Iron Age round house. Who were these people? We suggest young women and children. In the cattle-obsessed culture of early medieval Ireland, it was young women who went with the herds to the *macha samraid* – the summer milking place in the hills – and engaged in butter making (Kelly 1997, 450; Patterson 1994, 90-1; Ó Corráin 1972, 54). In the cattle transhumance practices of later historical

Ireland, it was also young women who drove the cattle herds to the summer pastures in the mountains and marshlands (Lucas 1989, 58-67). There they lived in booley huts from May to November, milking the cows and making cheeses that children would carry the short distance back down to the lowland settlements. Young men would occasionally also visit the booley site and the useful social distance that these places had from the normal world enabled young courting couples to try out various conjugal relationships before the winter marrying season (Patterson 1994). So, a social interpretation of the Iron Age houses at Goldcliff might be that their distinctive architecture signalled specific social and gender relationships that were embedded in, or were intrinsic to, the seasonal rhythms of economic activity in the estuarine wetlands.

Conclusion

This chapter has explored what could be considered to be the most important contribution that wetland archaeology can make to mainstream archaeological debate, that is the unsurpassed insights it gives into the dynamic nature of past people's lives. High-resolution and absolute dating techniques which require the survival of organic remains have offered unequalled understanding of the temporality of people's material culture in the widest sense. This ranges from the landscapes that wetland people inhabited, and the settlements they constructed, changed and abandoned, to the artefacts they made with their individual biographies and life-cycles. These frequently appear to be metaphorically linked to the lives of the people, and thus provide opportunities to explore the meaning of things from the perspective of the people we are trying to understand.

5

Politics and practice in wetland archaeology

Introduction

Most archaeologists would now agree that their investigation of past societies, their interpretation of landscapes and material culture, and their work in universities, government institutions and the commercial world is not carried out in a socio-political vacuum. Archaeologists, like everybody else, read newspapers, have political opinions, vote in elections, and practise their profession within a particular set of political and social relations (e.g. Johnson 1999). Indeed, some have long argued that archaeology itself as a cultural practice has always been and remains political (Shanks & Tilley 1987, 212). Interestingly, it could be argued that wetland archaeology, despite its long involvement in conservation and environmental debates, has been slow to recognise the political context of its work. Wetland archaeologists have generally shown reluctance to get involved in the types of political campaigns and controversies that their colleagues have been active in, reflecting their pragmatic functional approach.

We suggest that it is time to reflect on, and debate, the politics and practice of wetland archaeology. It is certainly true that wetland archaeologists have long been involved in the 'green issues' of the environmental and conservation debates, arguably long before other archaeologists began to think about such heritage management issues (B. Coles & Olivier 2001).

119

But how does this relate to local people? Do wetland archaeologists work for the preservation of waterlogged anaerobic soils that wondrously preserve archaeological deposits, but perhaps pay less attention to contemporary communities of the wetlands? It is encouraging that the 2003 WARP international wetland archaeology conference in Olympia, Washington, had several sessions devoted to wetlands and indigenous communities. This chapter will consider examples in the relationship of wetland archaeologists with local people, and also their relationship with those other 'guardians of the wetlands', the nature conservationists. It will also explore some ways that wetland archaeologists might begin to work in broader social and political terms.

Wetland archaeologists as reluctant politicians

The Iraqi marshlands

An illustration of this can be provided by a brief look at recent political campaigns relating to cultural heritage on the Rivers Tigris and Euphrates in Turkey and Iraq in the Middle East. In the early 1990s, with international financial assistance, the Turkish government began the South East Anatolia Project, a line of twenty-two dams which many believe will ultimately choke off the waters of these rivers. The World Archaeology Congress (WAC) raised a storm of protest, focusing on the Illisu Dam which they claimed would flood and destroy the landscapes and cultural heritage of the Kurdish people. After protests and effective campaigning, the British government was forced to withdraw its funding for this project.

Ironically, while 'wetlands' (i.e. dammed lakes) were being created in Turkey, further downstream the world-famous southern Iraqi marshlands on the Tigris and Euphrates were being drained. One of the world's most spectacular wetland cultural landscapes was being transformed and the ultimate

11. A *mudhif*, or guesthouse, in the marshlands of Iraq, utilising wetland products to express social identity (from the archive of Sir Wilfrid Thesiger; © Pitt Rivers Museum, Oxford).

'people of the wetlands' – the Madan or Marsh Arabs – were being oppressed and their cultural heritage destroyed. The Marsh Arabs are best known to western observers through the writings of travellers such as Wilfrid Thesiger. He described in the 1950s a people who lived on reed islands, built architecturally-spectacular communal meeting houses (*mudhif*) of dried reeds, fished and hunted from long canoes (*mashuf*), grew rice and kept water buffaloes in the marshes (Thesiger 1959, 1964; Maxwell 1957; Young 1977). This was a way of life that is often (perhaps inaccurately) described as thousands of years old, as the ancient histories of Sumer describe the region, the *mudhif* and the *mashuf*. However, as many wetland communities have experienced elsewhere, the Marsh Arabs were regarded with distrust by the Iraqi government, who saw the marshes as a refuge for bandits, smugglers and rebels disdainful of external control, and as bases for Shi'ite resistance groups (Lamb 2003).

121

After the unsuccessful Shi'ite rebellions immediately following the First Gulf War, the Iraqi government constructed rivers, canals and drains across the marshes, while the marsh villages were bombed and its peoples expelled. By 2001, most (i.e. 85%) of the Hammar and al-Qurnah marshes had been drained, while the al-Huwaizah marsh on the Iran border was also degraded (Lamb 2003, 26). Since the collapse of the Saddam Hussein government in 2004, the Marsh Arabs have become a focus of much NGO and charitable organisation activity, and engineering attempts are beginning to reflood the marshes. Ironically, it is probably too late to preserve the traditional culture of the Marsh Arabs, as young people have migrated to the region's towns and cities, preferring mobile phones and satellite TVs to the world of water buffaloes and reeds. The region's marshlands probably face a further threat in the growing interest of oil companies in the extensive oil resources under the marshes (Nicholson & Clark 2002).

It might have been expected that wetland archaeologists, who have frequently referred in their lectures and writings to the life and culture of the Marsh Arabs, would organise a protest campaign, write to newspapers or even comment on the destruction of a way of life that would seem to embody every-thing that they are fascinated by. It must surely also be the case that spectacularly preserved wetland archaeological sites testifying to thousands of years of inhabitation in the legendary Mesopotamian marshes were destroyed by this drainage. However, wetland archaeologists raised barely a peep of protest, and the reader will hunt in vain for any comment about this disaster in contemporary conference proceedings, monographs or articles published through the 1990s.

The Ramsar Convention addressed the cultural heritage of wetlands through its World Wetlands Day in 2002, which had as its theme 'Wetlands, Water, Life and Culture'; but prior to this, the heritage of people was considered only of secondary

122

importance compared to the nature conservation needs of the area. The World Wetlands Day drew attention to the fact that around the world, in the Middle East, India, Africa, Cambodia and the Americas (e.g. Costa Rica, Ecuador), indigenous wetland communities are under pressure from drainage programmes, development and even political, economic and military oppression. But the role of archaeology in protecting and sustaining present wetland communities is a topic that has rarely been addressed by archaeologists. The question could be asked, then: are wetland archaeologists interested only in the long-dead 'people of the wetlands'? If we accept a separation of the present from the past, as the politically reluctant wetland archaeologist might do, the answer to this question could well be 'yes'.

Archaeologists, locals and druids: a case study of 'Seahenge', England

While the Marsh Arabs of Southern Iraq may be a usefully distant, ethnographically exotic culture that wetland archaeologists can quote without getting involved in the politics of the region, they have also recently been caught on the hop by events closer to (our) home. Most archaeologists were probably surprised by the public response to the discovery of the Bronze Age timber circle at Holme, in North Norfolk, England – a site probably better known as Seahenge. Whilst arguably not carried out as a self-consciously wetland archaeology project, the site definitely drew much of its resonance and consequently its popular appeal from its seemingly liminal location on the intertidal zone of Norfolk's coastal wetlands and the remarkable quality of preservation of its waterlogged timbers. The response of most archaeologists to the Seahenge events would probably be to hold their heads in horror at the bitter controversy and media scrum that ensued. However, it is arguable that this will now be the reality of life for many archaeologists who, some might say, have long since crossed the line between being on the side of environmentalists and anti-development protesters to siding with the planning authorities and the government establishment. There are lessons in Seahenge for all archaeologists, wetland or not.

The Early Bronze Age timber circle at Holme consisted of the lower portion of an oak tree stump that had its roots removed and had been placed in an inverted position in a pit in the ground (Brennand & Taylor 2003). It was surrounded by a closely-spaced enclosure or 'circle' of cleft oak posts with their bark surfaces to the outside. Dendrochronological dating indicated that the tree stump was taken from a large oak tree that had been felled in spring 2050 BC, while the cleft posts were felled in 2049 BC. A rope of honeysuckle was found wrapped around the upside-down stump, and was possibly used to drag it into position. The site was originally located in a saltmarsh near to the coast, and was subsequently inundated under peats formed in fen conditions. Other finds from the immediate vicinity include bronze palstaves, Bronze Age pottery and smashed stones.

Interpretations of the Holme timber circle function vary, but it was almost certainly a ritual site, perhaps used for excarnation of corpses. Undoubtedly also, the inverted tree represented some aspect of the world turned upside down, while the whole structure may have been metaphorical for the inside and outside surfaces of a tree itself. Although popularly associated with the famous Stonehenge site, it is probably more closely related to the many Late Neolithic/Early Bronze Age timber circles found around Britain and Ireland, but with one startling difference: here survived not only post-holes but the posts themselves.

The rescue excavation of the Holme timber circle was to lead to one of the most hotly-disputed, high-profile archaeological research projects of recent decades, ultimately involving

5. Politics and practice in wetland archaeology

archaeologists, local communities, spiritualists, healers and modern druids (Champion 2000). The site was discovered in 1998, when John Lorimer, a local man out 'crabbing' on the beach, first picked up a bronze palstave on the intertidal zone, then noted the presence of an oak stump and posts set in an eroding bank of peats. He contacted the Norfolk Archaeological Unit which, excited by the site's potential, carried out a trial excavation, noted the presence of bronze axe toolmarks on the timbers and removed a large dendrochronological sample, which was to be seen later as an act of 'sacrilege'. The initial reaction of the archaeological authorities, notably English Heritage, was that the site would be too expensive to investigate, so that the best response should be to monitor the site's erosion into the sea, recording it as it went. However, the archaeological community, represented in particular by the Council for British Archaeology and its president, the wetland archaeologist Francis Pryor, argued strongly both through academic circles and the media that this was too significant an opportunity to be passed up and that the site had to be investigated fully.

English Heritage, under pressure, then agreed to fund archaeological excavations of the site and to remove the timbers for study and conservation. This position was also supported by the Norfolk Wildlife Trust, who were strongly concerned that the waders and breeding bird colonies of the local Holme Dunes, a National Nature Reserve, a Site of Special Scientific Interest (SSSI) and a Wetland of International Importance under the Ramsar Convention, were being adversely affected by public interest and activity on the site. At this stage, local and national media discovered that not everybody wanted the timber circle lifted. In particular, many within the local community of Holme wanted the site left alone and believed that the timber circle in a sense 'belonged' to the village and that it should not be removed from the landscape where in had been for thousands of years. Despite this local opposition, the archaeological authorities, believing that the site was doomed to destruction due to foreshore peat erosion, proposed to go on with the site excavations in May 1999. By now, the local protesters had been swelled by environmentalists, British Druids and spiritualists, who believed that the site's disturbance was a violent and unnecessary intervention into a sacred place and who attempted to halt the excavations, both through occupation of the site and through (failed) legal action. By June 1999, the excavations had resumed, partly through English Heritage's successful legal injunction against some of the protesters. Earthmoving machinery was brought onto the beach to enable the tree-stump to be hoisted out of the beach, providing the media, including the popular television series *Time Team*, with striking, even iconic photographs of massive machines poised over seemingly fragile and vulnerable timbers. The timbers were removed for conservation and study to the Flag Fen research centre, and have recently been the subject of academic publication, while their ultimate fate remains to be resolved (Brennand & Taylor 2003).

Whatever one's opinion of the events at Seahenge, it is undeniable that it was one of the most controversial archae-ological projects of recent years. Through the summer of 1999, the site became familiar to newspaper readers and television watchers (including those of us in Ireland), as it was used by the media as a *cause célèbre*. As outside observers and like many other archaeologists, we can only admit to being relieved that we were not personally involved or responsible for making difficult decisions about the site's future. Undoubtedly, many of the problems that ensued through that summer were due to poor communications between authorities and the local community and the involvement of an excitable media. It should also be recognised that this conflict may have been ultimately irresolvable, as archaeologists ironically found themselves trying to 'save' the site, while locals and druids accused them of 'destroying' the site. It is likely that any future similar discoveries will be allowed to simply erode into the sea, as once-bitten archaeologists will be too shy to go through it all again.

Whose (wetland) archaeology is it anyway?

This raises the question, how should wetland archaeologists work with local communities? It is arguable that we have been working closely with local communities long before post-processual writers urged an engagement with such people (e.g. Hodder 1999). Many years ago, Bryony and John Coles suggested that wetland archaeologists working in the Somerset Levels had to do their most important fieldwork in local pubs (B. & J. Coles 1986). He argued that it was only though talking with local men working on the peat-cutting machines, or with Somerset farmers working on the fields of the Levels, that archaeologists could establish the location of discoveries of previously hidden wooden structures and finds and to ensure their protection or excavation. Indeed, many of the well-known Somerset Levels trackways, for example the Sweet Track and Baker platform, are named after local men who first drew attention to them, and the history of archaeological discovery on the Levels reflects its agricultural development. Wetland archaeologists can only rarely draw on aerial photography and geophysical surveys, and 'local knowledge' remains of prime importance. Indeed, in our own careers working on bog trackways, lakes and estuarine levels, it was often local informants who drew our attention to previously unknown archaeological sites (e.g. Raftery 1996; Van de Noort 2004b). The presence of wetland archaeologists living and working in local villages during projects has also commonly led to the growth of local interest in archaeological heritage, typically supported by the programmes of lectures to local historical and community groups and to university extra-mural classes, site open-days, newspaper and radio interviews that many of us have engaged in. By and large, though, this activity has typically been accidental and unplanned, rather than carried out after careful reflection.

Community archaeology: archaeologists working with 'people of the wetland' in Britain and Ireland

In recent years, some archaeologists have attempted to establish more formal and informal relations with local communities. In her recent research programme on the crannogs of Lough Gara, Co. Sligo, in north-west Ireland, the Swedish archaeologist Christina Fredengren chose first to approach the local community and ask whether they would be willing to have her work on the local archaeology for her PhD in the University of Stockholm (Fredegren 2002). Enthusiastically received, she then lived and worked in the village of Monasteraden over a period of some five years, directing surveys and excavations. Throughout the project, Fredengren included the local community in her work, occasionally employing young people on site excavations and leading well-attended public visits to the archaeological sites. The strong local interest in the project is reflected in the size of the attendance at art exhibitions inspired by the research and the launch of the project's final monograph.

In this publication, Fredengren argues that she aimed to use the crannog archaeology to enable local people to construct identities that would empower them to resist the loss of sense of community, place and time that is the result of globalisation. However, as with any community project, she recognises that people will insist on multiple and conflicting views of the past. Indeed, she revealingly notes her own disappointment when local people refused to speak the language of 'postmodernism' in the script of a village monument celebrating the lake's archaeology (Fredengren 2002). It could be suggested then that there is always an inherent problem with outside academics and professional archaeologists telling people how to think about their heritage in any landscape, whether it be a wetland one or not. Nonetheless, Fredengren's project was an exciting and innovative one, opening up new ways of working with the past and local communities.

The case of Sutton Common, South Yorkshire, UK

The excavations of the Iron Age marsh fort at Sutton Common, in South Yorkshire, offered similar opportunities to the local community. The Sutton Common site is located near Askern, where economic prosperity has been badly affected by the recent closure of the coal mine and coking plant. Apart from such characteristics as high unemployment and low entry levels to higher education, a distinct lack of pride of place existed here. From within the local community (channelled through the Askern Community Partnership – now the North Doncaster Rural Trust), courageous attempts have been made to lift the community's self-esteem, and the excavations at Sutton Common were to play a key role in this. Excavations of this site, comprising two large enclosures on either side of a palaeochannel, have been the subject of excavations since the 1880s (e.g. Whiting 1936; Parker Pearson & Sydes 1996), but this research was undertaken from outside the local community. In 1997 the land was bought by the Carstairs Countryside Trust with help from English Heritage and the Heritage Lottery Fund with the aim of managing this desiccating wetland site, and the involvement of the local community was established that same year.

After initial small-scale archaeological evaluations in 1998 and 1999, English Heritage decided to sponsor much larger-scale excavations of the larger of the two enclosures, an area in excess of five acres. In the project design for the excavations, the local community was offered access and a degree of owner-ship to the site and research by providing access and training to local volunteers; an on-site education programme for local primary and secondary schools; an 'open door' policy in accepting visitors on site whilst excavations were ongoing, and formal 'open days' at the end of each campaign. A free conference held in the Askern Miners' Welfare building and a popular book on the site and its landscape (Smith 2004), both organised and produced in close co-operation with the North Doncaster Rural Trust, complement this approach to community archaeology. From a local perspective, the excavations offered a vehicle for refocusing attention on the local environment. Future plans involve the construction of a multi-functional community centre on the edge of Sutton Common that incorporates heritage facilities for visitors and training opportunities for local people. As excavators (the project was directed by RVdN), it was particularly interesting to note the hugely supportive feedback and help in many forms received from local people, and the complete absence of any acts of vandalism to the excavations or our campsite that had been experienced by previous excava-tors here. In fact, we attribute the non-appearance of 'night hawking' metal detectorists to the vigilance of local people and their sense of ownership of the Iron Age marsh fort.

Using the excavations at Sutton Common as a springboard, an additional project was designed to inspire and raise the aspirations of local schoolchildren: Rubbish and Archaeology. It involved the burial of items of lunch waste selected by the schoolchildren, ranging from cheese sandwiches to crisps, and from a vacuum-packed sausage to a locally caught perch, side-by-side with experimental archaeological objects such as legs of lamb, trout, wheat, leather, wood, metal, basketry and replica pottery (Van de Noort & Panter 2001). All items were analysed prior to burial and after excavation using a range of standard archaeological tools, including digital photography, chromatic sensor and video microscope. The principles of what archaeology is, and what happens to rubbish in a modern world, were clearly illustrated to the pupils by their engagement with these basic taphonomic studies. Working alongside archaeologists, we hope to have demystified academic pursuits, at least to some degree. And in any case, the project was fun and informative to all involved.

Tribe-archaeological co-operation in cultural and scientific wet site investigations – Ozette and the Qwu?gwes Wet Site, Washington State

There have been even more exciting breakthroughs in the integration of archaeologists with local communities during wetland projects. Perhaps this is most evident where there is a clear distinction in ethnic and cultural identities such as between the descendants of European colonists and native peoples in North America. For years, archaeologists from around the world have watched the often troublesome relationships between North American archaeologists and First Nations groups, and the bitter controversies over reburial and excavations are well-known.

Wetland archaeologists in the USA and Canada are currently at the foreground of establishing new types of mutually beneficial relationships with First Nations. Arguably one of the earliest of these originated during the archaeological excavations in the 1970s of a wet site at Ozette, in the remote north-western tip of the Olympic Peninsula on the Pacific north-west coast of Washington State. This is the homeland of the Makah Nation, whose name translates as 'the people who live by the rocks and seagulls', who have traditionally lived by fishing and whaling. Beginning with the Ozette excavations, the Makah Nation gained momentum in the revitalisation of their language and culture and built a Makah Cultural and Research Centre at Neah Bay, at the core of which is an astonishing museum devoted to the traditional culture and lifeways of the people. The ancient origins of these lifeways has been partly confirmed by the Ozette wet site archaeological excavations. For example, a crucially important piece of evidence that proved that the Makah Nation had used nets in salmon fishing, which the modern state authorities were trying to ban, was provided by well-preserved net fragments from these pre-contact site excavations. It had previously been argued by the authorities that nets were a European introduction. However, the Makah Cultural and Research Centre could be considered as more than a mere museum that reflects the classic interests of colonial powers. It is an 'autoethnography', a self portrait of the Makah people, who have selected elements of European culture – archaeology, museology and linguistics – to express and continue Makah identity (Pierce Erikson 2002, 99-142).

In recent years, the Squaxin Island tribe of Washington have been working closely with anthropologists from South Puget Sound Community College of Washington State University (Foster & Croes 2002; Croes & Foster 2004). At a time when many North American archaeologists find it difficult to give a real voice to local tribal and First Nations groups, this highly innovative programme of work was actually built on a formal, 50/50 cooperative agreement signed by tribal elders, archaeological authorities and heads of the educational institution. This has led to anthropologists and tribal members working together to create scientific and cultural results that both require.

That formal cooperative agreement led to the formation of a Cultural Resource Management Office amongst the Squaxin Island tribe, so that the tribe could be involved in the writing of cultural histories. It has also enabled an innovative Outreaching Training programme, using online teaching methods and resources, to enable young tribal members to receive college

12. Qwu?gwes tribal basket weavers Rhonda Foster (left) and Barbara Henry (right) discuss the composition of an ancient Squaxin basket (courtesy of Dale Croes).

training in archaeological methods. Perhaps most excitingly, this agreement has also encouraged the establishment of an archaeological field school at a pre-contact site, Qwu?gwes (also known as Mud Bay), where there have been investigations of a village/town living area, a waterlogged, intertidal midden (with the discovery of a cedar bark gill net), an inshore cedar stake fishtrap, and a nineteenth-century Euro-American homestead. Much of the technological interpretation of the artefacts recovered has been provided by tribal elders, with their store of knowledge of traditional practices (Croes & Foster 2003). Finally there is also a Squaxin Island museum, library and research centre that provides local communities, whether they be of First Nations or Euro-American background, with a considerable cultural resource.

So if we ask ourselves 'whose (wetland) archaeology is it

anyway?', then the answer is clearly that archaeologists, professional or otherwise, and local communities have at least equal rights to this aspect of the past, and through the case studies presented here we have shown that there is clearly a potential future for wetland archaeology in terms of community archaeology. Whilst this is true for all archaeology, in the wetland context the archaeological invisibility of the past and the potential impact of actions beyond the boundaries of the site, especially in terms of hydrology, require such co-operation if we want to find and preserve the archaeological resource. How might this be achieved? It is likely that wetland archaeologists interested in community projects should aim to establish communication with local groups at an early stage, with an emphasis on the writing of collaborative regional cultural histories presented in a plain, easily understood fashion. Such projects should also aim to incorporate archaeological findings with folklore and the insights provided in local, oral historical narratives. Community projects should also aim for the employment and training of local people, so as to empower local communities in the interpretation of their own histories. Finally, community projects should aim for continuous public presentations (lectures, exhibitions, workshops), the establishment of locally available photographic and video archives and educational resources, and a community involvement in tourism and heritage merchandising, and this has now become embedded in official policies for wetland archaeology (e.g. Olivier & Van de Noort 2002). Indeed, the lessons of the projects described above indicate that this should involve alliances between local communities and research institutions.

Wetland archaeology and nature conservation

In the relationship of wetland archaeology with environmental protection we notice an increased concurrence of archaeological and nature conservation interests, but the relationships between the practitioners involved has not always been one of mutual co-operation. Indeed, a not-so distant conference at Bristol in 1994, entitled *Wetlands: archaeology and nature conservation* (Cox *et al.* 1995) was billed as exploring the differences between the two groups. Participants will vividly remember the moment when one well-respected nature conservationist accused wetland archaeologists of colluding with the peat diggers and extractors in order to further their own careers. The ensuing heated argument raised a number of issues that exposed unjust preconceptions in both groups and, paradoxically, may be considered in hindsight as representing a turning point in their relationship. So what were these differences?

First, there was the debate on what the term wetlands actually meant. We have already argued in Chapter 2 that the term 'wetlands' is of recent date, and that it has had different meanings for archaeologists and nature conservationists: for archaeologists, wetlands are landscapes that preserve organic remains through waterlogging, while for nature conservationists they are usually seen as peatlands, especially lowland raised mires in the 1990s, but increasingly also river valleys. Thus few nature conservationists consider the whole of the East Anglian Fenlands as a wetland, in stark contrast to the archaeologists who work there, and such a discrepancy cannot form the basis for successful co-operation to preserve this landscape as a wetland. In most countries, archaeologists are on their own in their attempts to protect the archaeology of minerogenic wetlands, which are typically under intensive arable agriculture and therefore of little value to nature conservation. Similar situations exist for a number of French, German and Swiss lake villages, where the demands of development related to tourism add to the lack of support for conservation of the historic environment (e.g. Fisher *et al.* 2004). Conversely, archaeologists have focused their campaigns for the protection of peatlands on areas with well known archaeological sites, rather than supporting the protection of all peatlands *per se*, or even the 'best' peatlands in an ecological sense.

Secondly, archaeologists have dealt with threats to wetland sites *reactively*, with rescue excavations and surveys carried out as a result of those threats, contrasting with the more *proactive* approach taken by nature conservationists seeking legislative protection for the most important peatlands. We must also consider here the fact that when trackways or other archaeological sites are damaged by activities such as peat digging, opportunities arise for archaeologist to excavate and study the site (or 'preserve it by record' rather than *in situ*). In the Somerset Levels, the peat extractors actively supported the archaeologists with information exchange and access, and in the Irish Midlands archaeological research and rescue excavations have been financed and practically supported by Bord na Móna, the Irish state body devoted to the mining of Irish boglands. Whilst some archaeologists see such support as reasonable and acceptable mitigation of the damage caused to the archaeological resource, according to the 'polluter pays' principle, from the point of view of nature conservationists, such a collaboration looked like treachery, in which archaeologists actively gained their information from wetland destruction. Obviously, the point could be made here that nature conservation professionals equally made their careers out of the threats to wetlands, but their work involved confronting those organisations that damaged wetlands rather than collaborating with them.

Thirdly, whilst archaeologists seek a *status quo* in terms of land-use and hydrology, nature conservationists need a dynamic environment that is capable of sustaining particular flora and fauna identified by them as being of significance, for example in order to achieve biodiversity targets. Traditionally, to preserve organic archaeological remains *in situ*, preferred conditions are those that are least changeable. For example, it is widely thought that a strongly fluctuating watertable accelerates microbial activity and thus the humification of any organic remains. Similarly bioturbation, including root activity, has been identified as potentially damaging. However, wetlands are by definition dynamic landscapes which, without management, will evolve naturally through hydroseral succession or other such processes.

Fourthly, archaeologists have tended to concentrate on small-scale areas (about the size of an archaeological site), while the nature conservation interest involved the larger scale (the whole ecosystem). During the 1994 Bristol conference, archaeologists accused nature reserve managers of damaging the fragile organic archaeological remains when they excavated small amounts of peat to create bunds to dam up drainage ditches, thus reversing the drainage of large mires. The conservationists' reaction was one of total bewilderment. Surely, it was argued, the preservation of whole mire ecosystems is more important that the preservation of a small archaeological site?

In addition to these arguments, we recognise a debate for the moral high ground of wetland protection. The dispute involved such questions as 'how natural/cultural are wetlands?' and 'who is really the guardian of the wetlands?' These differences were further exacerbated by the fact that almost everywhere, separate organisations have responsibility for archaeological conservation/heritage management and nature conservation, and we also recognise that in terms of broader public support, financial assistance and legislative protection, archaeology nearly always loses out to nature conservation. Because of the separated funding systems supporting archaeology and nature conservation, any co-operation therefore frequently involves cumbersome management structures, steering committees and overseeing panels. The ability to respond unilaterally to any threats to wetlands or wetland archaeological sites is therefore more practicable than relying on agreements from multiple organisations, each with their own rules on transparency, accountability and value-for-money. This is not to say that archaeologists have not been able to co-operate with nature conservationists. For example, co-operation on Shapwick Heath preserved extensive parts of the Sweet Track *in situ* (B. Coles 1995), but the fact that this example is frequently mentioned in the literature indicates its exceptional status.

Over the last decade, explicit attempts have been made to build bridges, and on the basis of existing co-operation on the ground, to establish high-level frameworks that enable further multi-agency work. In England, for example, the co-operation between archaeological and nature conservation organisations has been explicitly identified in the *English Heritage Strategy for Wetlands* as being crucial for the future of wetland management (Olivier & Van de Noort 2002). We also note recent co-operative projects elsewhere, for example in the protection of the Federsee lake settlement in southern Germany, and elsewhere in Europe numerous individual examples can be seen to have developed, even if they do not yet amount to a widespread practice (see B. Coles & Olivier 2001; J. Coles 2004). So what has changed?

In essence, most of the issues of conflict that existed in the early 1990s have been resolved. For example, the broader use of the term 'wetlands' is now widely accepted by nature conservation organisations, and recent floods of river floodplains in western Europe have refocused the attention of governments on these minerogenic wetlands. Also, archaeologists increasingly adopt a proactive stance to wetland management, accepting that the protection of whole wetland landscapes also means the protection of any archaeological sites contained within them, even if we cannot identify these sites. An increasing acceptance that the peat itself is an archaeological record further reinforces the proactive approach. As part of this shift in thinking, archaeologists progressively accept that dynamic wetlands can provide the protection they have yearned for; after all, it was dynamic wetlands (and not fossilised ones) that preserved the Sweet Track, Corlea 1, Flag Fen, Seahenge and all those other sites we treasure. We have also noticed an improvement in the general attitude towards the people and organisations that damage wetlands, including peat extractors, farmers and drainage boards. Today, we recognise the many 'stakeholders' in this debate, and the collaboration-or-confrontation argument is no longer a valid one. Practical problems in co-operation remain, but these are no longer seen as preventing it. The need for joined-up government has now become widely accepted. Perhaps both wetland conservationists and archaeologists (in Europe and America) also need to join up their thinking on 'whose wetland heritage it is anyway' – in other words, they need to clarify their views on the rights of the local communities who live in, work and culturally 'own' these wetland landscapes today.

Conclusion

This chapter has explored the role of wetland archaeologists and their engagement with current political debates. The richness of the material of the past in wetlands has tended to focus the archaeologist's mind on the sites and finds themselves (this trackway, that bog body), rather than on broader issues such as the conservation of whole wetland landscapes, concern for the current people of the wetlands, and interaction with, and empowerment of, local people vis-à-vis their heritage. However, we have also noted recent changes in these matters, and specific wetland projects can now be named as leading the way in offering best practice examples in multi-agency co-operation and in the involvement of local people – not only in the study of the past, but also in the enrichment of the present.

6

Conclusion

The modern traveller to past wetlands: description or understanding?

Travel has often been seen as a useful metaphor for how we explore past worlds. In a famous and evocative phrase, the novelist and literary critic, L.P. Hartley, suggested that 'the past is a foreign country, they do things differently there'. However, archaeologists, historians and anthropologists have long known that we cannot simply travel back to the past (or to present worlds), witness people's words and actions and assume that that is the way things were. In that vein, anthropologists have long tried to deal with the interpretative challenges facing the travelling ethnographer, developing the concept of the 'participant observer'; the person who interprets other people's worlds while recognising their own involvement in the process. Dealing with the same problem, Clifford Geertz (1983) suggested that anthropologists can usefully reflect on the difference between 'experience near' (i.e. people's local knowledge and their own intimate experience and understanding of their society) and 'experience distant' (i.e. the scientific scholar's perceptions as an outsider). Geertz (2000, 16) suggested that the study of other peoples' cultures involved discovering who people thought they were, what they thought they were doing and to what end they thought they were doing it.

How have wetland archaeologists travelled to the past? We suggest that Wilfrid Thesiger's *The Marsh Arabs* (1964) provides a good analogy. The book describes Thesiger's travels

6. Conclusion

in southern Iraq between 1951 and 1958, providing an unparalleled description of the best-known 'people of the wetlands' surviving into the twentieth century. Using chapter headers such as 'A Glimpse of the Marshes', 'First Impressions of the Madan', 'Winning Acceptance' and 'My Last Year in the Marshes', this archetypal English explorer details the architecture, economy, traditions and beliefs of this distinctive community. The enduring popularity of the book lies, at least in part, in the story-telling which appeals to the adventurer in ourselves. Thesiger makes no apologies for this approach. As he states himself in the introduction, 'I spent these years in the Marshes because I enjoyed being there' (Thesiger 1964, 1).

We believe that this feeling – that we do the research because we enjoy it – would be expressed by many of our wetland archaeological colleagues and, indeed, ourselves. Speaking from our personal experiences, the years spent exploring the archaeology of the Humber, Severn and Shannon estuaries, leading fieldtrips into the Somerset Levels, digging prehistoric bog trackways in Corlea, and simply 'dwelling', as Tilley (2004, 219) would have it, in the lakes of Midlands Ireland, have been among the highlights of our professional lives. Other wetland archaeologists have similarly reflected on the impact on their lives of the silence and feeling of peace in the middle of a raised mire, and on the excitement and joy when excavating fragile prehistoric artefacts that looked and felt as if they had been made yesterday. Though it is unfashionable to say so now, there is no excitement like that moment when you observe a sharpened wooden post and realise, in that instant, that the last person to see its perfectly preserved toolmarks was the man or woman who hammered it into the ground thousands of years ago. That the wetlands we worked in were the kinds of landscapes avoided by most people in modern society reinforced that feeling of specialness and belonging. No doubt this is an inheritance that comes from a number of sources: the nineteenth-century Roman-

13. Wetlands as taskscapes: the Madan fishing in a traditional manner, providing fish for the markets of Baghdad (from the archive of Sir Wilfrid Thesiger; © Pitt Rivers Museum, Oxford).

tic movement's belief in the 'wildness' of nature, the more recent work of twentieth-century poets, artists and others, such as Seamus Heaney's work on bogs, and perhaps too our own postmodern, ontological anxieties about placelessness and the disconnection from the perceived simplicities and pastoral rhythms of the rural lives lived by our ancestors.

To a degree, aspects of Thesiger's work are mirrored by the efforts of many archaeologists working in wetlands in the last four decades. The fragility of the wetland landscapes and the archaeological remains provide an unambiguous justification for directing research funding to wetlands. Thesiger's observation that 'soon the Marshes will probably be drained; when this happens, a way of life that has lasted for thousands of years will disappear' (ibid.) could be repeated for many other wetlands, even if the traditional ways of life revealed in them had disappeared long before our arrival. Nevertheless, the need for rapid action in recording such fragile remains provides a validation for the extensive rescue projects that take place in many countries in western Europe and elsewhere (see Coles 2001).

Thesiger attempted to give a 'picture of the Marshes and of the people who live here' (ibid.). His work is principally ethnographical, retaining his position as an outsider and focusing on description, rather than ethnological, which aims for deeper understanding of the society that he was part of for nearly a decade. Again, we recognise that this positivist, descriptive approach has been adopted by many others who have been awed by wetland landscapes. Might it not be true that wetland archaeologists like Thesiger, who was notoriously suspicious of modern technologies and theories, have also revelled in the description of material culture, rather than its deeper interpretation? Thesiger's work is full of respect for these people's ingenuity, their way of life and above all its distance from the modern world, to some extent elevating the noble aspects of the 'primitive' society he studied. It is perhaps the case that wetland archaeology's similar fascination with the practical aspects of past people's lifeways springs from a similar distrust of theory. After all, who needs fancy models, convoluted theories or complicated interpretations, when the archaeology is there in front of us and speaks for itself, but under constant and imminent threat of destruction?

The answer is, of course, we do! Wetland archaeologists are part of a wider community, that of archaeology, which has its own progressive development in aims, objectives, methods and techniques. Description without understanding cannot be the ultimate objective of our work, even where the research is rescue-based; and if excavators themselves fail to reach for this understanding, their wetland surveys and excavations are simply not contributing to archaeology to the degree that their efforts warrant. In order to achieve this, we need to refocus our theoretical outlook and reintegrate wetland archaeology with mainstream archaeology.

A new theoretical focus

During the last four decades, wetland archaeology has been undertaken first and foremost from a functionalist paradigm. As already argued in Chapter 1, the functionalist archaeologist looks for 'common sense' answers, and in practice this means the search for answers within an economic functionalism. With the abundance of environmental data available, such interpretations tend to lean towards environmental determinism. Frequently description is considered of greater value than interpretation, especially in the light of the threats that continue to damage the waterlogged sites. Typically, explicit theoretical considerations are omitted from our writings, and there is the underlying assumption that the spade (or the spatula) cannot lie. Of course, the spade itself cannot lie because it is the archaeologist who wields it who explains what has been uncovered. In other words, all archaeological data has to be interpreted, and this interpretation takes place from a basis of implicit or explicit theoretical beliefs (i.e. Matthew Johnson's 1999 'cloud of theory'). We have also argued that generalisation over too broad a geographical or temporal span is nearly always misleading, regardless of whether it is based on functionalist, processual or post-processual points of view. We have not sought to directly attack a modernist or processual wetland archaeology, as in actual fact this has never emerged as a significant way of thinking.

In the preceding chapters, we have presented a number of different kinds of interpretation. In Chapter 2 we advocated new ways of approaching wetland landscapes. In effect, we argued for an approach which puts the way in which people in the past perceived their own environments above one in which our modern understanding of wetlands is predominant. This includes the realisation that the concept of wetlands is a recent one, and that we must be more sensitive to the specificity of the types of wetland that was lived in by past people. We noted that trackways, such as the Sweet Track, were not merely built to provide a route across a wetland, but that the crossing itself was embedded with multiple meanings. The votive and structured depositions that have been found alongside many trackways are witness to this. In Chapter 3 we claimed that the people of the wetlands were individuals and groups actively engaged with their landscapes, with varied but frequently distinctive social identities, and who should no longer be understood as the pawns in the changing landscape and environment that determined their actions. For example, people used wetlands to express their remoteness from the rest of society by living on crannogs in Ireland, or by reinventing traditions to express links to the past as revealed by the study of fishtraps in the Shannon estuary. Chapter 4 explored the application of high-resolution dating to a new understanding of the dynamic nature of past people's lives. High-resolution and absolute dating techniques, which require the survival of organic remains, have offered an unequalled understanding of the temporality of material culture in the widest sense. We have argued that the dynamics of people's lives are reflected in the life-cycles of their material culture, which is shown in the Alpine lake settlements and in certain objects, providing new opportunities to explore the meaning of things from the perspective of the people we are trying to understand. Chapter 5 reconsidered the role that is played by us as archaeologists. We argued that we, like the people we study, are active agents and that the manner in which we interpret our data and engage with local communities and other individuals and organisations involved in wetlands is essentially a political one.

These different kinds of interpretation belong essentially to a postmodern way of thinking, and we consider that our re-engagement with mainstream archaeology can be most successfully achieved by adopting a number of the characteristics of this approach. We do not argue here for a rejection of the study of the economic functions of wetlands, as we obviously recognise that people in the past and present live in and off wetlands. We do, however, reject arguments in which the economic exploitation of these landscapes is seen as the be-all and end-all of wetland archaeology. Thus not only should marginality and productivity be economically defined, but the social, political and religious aspects of such concepts must be recognised. This study has shown on several occasions the inadequacy of any generalised meta-narrative of 'wetlands', and we have taken the view that, in order to gain a deep understanding of the interaction of past people with wetlands, we need to be sensitive to the specificity of the social, political, religious and economic aspects of the people we study.

Reintegrating wetland archaeology: a new way of working

The aim of this book is to rethink wetland archaeology so that it becomes fully integrated with mainstream archaeological debate, without losing the characteristics and benefits of working in different landscapes that have the ability to preserve organic remains. The way to achieve this involves four essential stages.

First, wetland archaeologists must equip themselves with a clear understanding of the broader issues current in archaeological debate. No sub-field or specialist area within archaeology should become isolated from the broader questions that are being addressed. Of course, wetland archaeologists are by no means the only specialists who find themselves in this situation, and alongside maritime and environmental archaeology, already mentioned as examples, many other fields within archaeology need to 'touch base' periodically. This requires participation through the range of events and activities that are

6. Conclusion

available to all, including conferences, publications and lectures. The purpose of global wetland archaeology conferences and specialist publications must be clearly defined if we want to reject the accusation of 'wetlandism'. Such global events clearly have a role to play. It is quite appropriate, for example, that wetland-specific excavation techniques, or the management of wetlands for archaeological preservation and conservation, should be addressed at such a forum. Certain material culture studies will also benefit from cross-cultural comparisons, especially where they involve technical aspects such as woodworking, or the weaving of basketry. Other wetland studies may provide inspiration to the initiated. But where global comparisons take precedence over contextualised studies, a rethink is clearly needed.

As the many case studies presented in this book have shown, the focus of our research does not necessarily need to shift from rescuing the sites that are under threat, but the academic objectives of any such rescue work must have significance and pertinence beyond the sub-field of wetland archaeology. We have shown that wetland archaeology can address current issues such as social identities, interaction with natural places, processes of enculturation, and agency. Clearer and more explicit statements of the theoretical viewpoint that forms the basis for the interpretations presented in wetland archaeology would assist in this integration.

Secondly, in designing our research and formulating our aims and objectives, we must recognise that wetlands cannot be treated as islands in the wider landscapes. Here we have presented a number of different case studies that show that 'the people of the wetlands' engaged actively with the physical landscapes beyond the wetland edge and with the people who lived there. And *vice versa*, people who did not live in wetlands themselves engaged actively or passively with these landscapes. The votive depositions in wet places and the bog bodies,

147

the trackways, the crannogs and the fishweirs can only be understood by taking a contextualised approach to wetlands, as illustrated by the examples presented in the previous chapters. We have also argued that we need to recognise the different types of wetlands rather than treating all wetlands as a homogeneous landscape group, and this could also help in developing integrated rather than isolated studies.

Whilst we concur with John Coles's (2001) analysis in his *Energetic Activities of Commoners* (J. Coles 2001; see also Chapter 1) of the strengths of wetland archaeology that must be exploited to the benefit of the wider archaeological debate, we believe that these key elements are too narrowly defined. For example, the first two of these key elements, environment & change and economy & subsistence, clearly reflect the functionalist background of wetland research described above. Whilst wetland archaeology is perfectly placed to advance debates on environmental change, economy and subsistence through the analysis of pollen, plant and invertebrate macrofossils integrated with cultural remains, this focus seems too restricted. Wetlands also contain 'added-value' archaeology on a range of other topics, for example the perception and understanding of 'landscapes at the edge' (whether in ideological or symbolic terms). Much has been written about the latter theme (i.e. sacred landscapes) in respect of votive depositions in 'wet places' (e.g. Bradley 1990), but this debate has taken place outside the community of wetland archaeologists who, as we shall argue later, have much to contribute to it. The fourth and sixth key elements, structures & activities and the range of material culture, are also generally recognised as important strengths in wetland archaeology. But we should not forget that people in the past and present have chosen to live in wetlands, and that such places actively created distinctive identities. Louwe Kooijmans' (1993) paper was based on this presumption, and many ancient wetland traditions survive in the modern world, such as the Madan in the Iraqi marshlands (Thesiger 1964) or the peoples of the Amazon basin (Harris 2000). Within such cultural traditions, particular identities have been constructed that are built around the daily interaction of the inhabitants with the dynamic landscapes of marsh and water. These identities were in turn expressed in the material culture of such wetland dwellers, ranging from the imposing reed-built *mudif* or guest house of the Iraqi marshlands to the status-indicating woven basketry hats on the north-west coast of North America (e.g. Croes 2001).

Thirdly, wetland archaeological research needs to be designed so that it addresses aspects of broader archaeological research and builds on its strengths. John Coles's third and fifth key elements of wetland archaeology, stratification & context and chronology & precision, may be used as an example here. Deep stratigraphies, built up in areas where sediment accumulates or peat overgrows sites, provide contexts of a quality that are not often found on the drylands. The advantages provided must be translated into real gains in knowledge and understanding for archaeology as a whole. The study of the lake settlements near the Bodensee (B. Coles 1999; Chapter 4), for example, provides an excellent basis to reconsider much of the settlement evidence from dryland contexts in the light of the concept of frequently shifting villages. As part of such analysis, Neolithic settlement patterns reconstructed for areas without high-precision dating should be revisited, and new hypotheses on the dynamic nature of Neolithic settlements can be developed.

The contribution of wetland archaeology can also lie in the illumination of the 'invisible people', the women and children who may have expressed their identities primarily through organic materials rather than through stone and pottery. One specific contribution lies in the appreciation of the 'special' character of many wetlands, which is important for any landscape study. This can be seen in the trackways that were

149

constructed into or across the wetlands and their associated finds, the bog bodies and votive depositions, and in the use of water and wetlands to define status and social marginality, as demonstrated by the crannogs of Ireland.

Fourthly, the result of this research must be disseminated widely and be made relevant to a broader audience. Only if the generic lessons of wetland research are disseminated to a broader audience – be they new insights into the past from the use of dendrochronological dating, or a greater understanding of the importance of organic material culture to past societies – will wetland archaeology regain a progressive position in archaeological studies. This, in turn, will improve the support, financial and otherwise, that wetland archaeology receives.

This, we submit, is our agenda for the future of wetland archaeology.

Bibliography

Appadurai, A. 1986. Introduction: commodities and the politics of value. In A. Appadurai (ed.) *The Social Life of Things: commodities in cultural perspective*, Cambridge University Press, Cambridge, 3-63

Arnold, B. 1986a. *Cortaillod-Est, un village du Bronze final*, Archeologie Neuchateloise 1, Saint Blaise

Arnold, B. 1986b. *Cortaillod-Est, un village du Bronze final*, Archeologie Neuchateloise 6, Saint Blaise

Arnold, B. 1990. Villages du Bronze Final sur les rives du Lac de Neuchatel. In C. Mordant & A. Richard (eds) *L'Habitat et l'occupation du sol a L'âge du Bronze en Europe*, 303-12, Lons-le-Saunier

Aston, M. & Burrow, I. (eds) 1982. *The Archaeology of Somerset: a review to 1500 AD*, Somerset County Council, Taunton

Barber, J.W. & Crone, B.A. 1993. Crannogs; a diminishing resource? A survey of southwest Scotland and excavations at Buiston crannog. *Antiquity* 67, 520-33

Barrett, J.C. 1994. *Fragments from Antiquity: an archaeology of social life in Britain, 2900 BC – 1200 BC*, Blackwell, Oxford

Barrett, J., Bradley, R. & Green, M. 1991. *Landscape, Monuments and Society: the prehistory of Cranborne Chase*. Cambridge University Press, Cambridge

Basso, K.H. 1996. *Wisdom Sits in Places: landscape and language among the western Apache*, University of New Mexico Press, Albuquerque

Bell, M. 1993a. Intertidal archaeology at Goldcliff in the Severn estuary. In J. Coles, V. Fenwick & G. Hutchinson (eds), *A Spirit of Enquiry. Essays for Ted Wright*, 9-13, WARP, Exeter

Bell, M. 1993b. Field survey and excavation at Goldcliff, Gwent 1993. *Archaeology in the Severn Estuary 1993*, 81-101

Bell, M. 1999. Prehistoric settlements and activities in the Welsh Severn Estuary. In B. Coles, J. Coles & M.S. Jørgensen (eds), *Bog Bodies, Sacred Sites and Wetland Archaeology*, 17-25, WARP, Exeter

Bell, M. 2003. Making one's way in the world: trackways from a wetland and dryland perspective. In D. Croes (ed.) *Wetland Archae-*

ology Research Project: 10th International Conference: Wet sites connections, April 1-5, 2003, Olympia, Washington: Conference Preprints, 1-18, Olympia

Bell, M., Caseldine, A. & Neumann, H. 2000. *Prehistoric Intertidal Archaeology in the Welsh Severn Estuary,* CBA Research Report 120, York

Bell, M. & Neumann, H. 1996. Intertidal survey in the Welsh Severn estuary. *Archaeology in the Severn Estuary 1995* 6, 29-33

Bell, M. & Neumann, H. 1997. Prehistoric intertidal archaeology and environments in the Severn estuary, Wales. *World Archaeology* 29 (1), 95-113

Bell, M. & Neumann, H. 1998. Intertidal survey in the Welsh Severn estuary. *Archaeology in the Severn Estuary 1997* 8, 13-28

Bender, B. 1998. *Stonehenge: making space,* Berg, Oxford

Bender, B. (ed.) 1993. *Landscape: politics and perspectives,* Berg, London

Bender, B. & Winer, M. (eds) 2001. *Contested Landscapes: landscapes of movement and exile,* Berg, Oxford

Bernick, K. 1988. Stylistic characteristics of basketry from Coast Salish area wet sites. In K. Bernick (ed.) *Hidden Dimensions: the cultural significance of wetland archaeology,* 139-56, University of British Columbia Press, Vancouver

Besteman, J.C. 1990. North Holland AD 400-1200: turning tide or tide turned? In J.C. Besteman, J.M. Bos & H.A. Heidinga (eds) *Medieval Archaeology in the Netherlands. Studies presented to H.H. van Regteren Altena,* 91-120, Van Gorcum, Assen/Maastricht

Bintcliff, J. (ed.) 1991. *The Annales School and Archaeology,* Leicester University Press, Leicester

Bocquet, A. & Huot, A. 1994. *Charavines il y a 5000 ans.* Editions Faton, Dijon

Bocquet, A. *et al.* 1987. A submerged Neolithic village: Charavines 'Les Baigneurs' in Lake Paladru, France. In J.M. Coles & A. Lawson (eds) *European Wetlands in Prehistory,* 33-54, Clarendon Press, Oxford

Bond, C.J. 2004. The Sweet Track, Somerset: a place mediating culture and spirituality?. In T. Insoll (ed.) *Belief in the Past. The Proceedings of the Manchester Conference on Archaeology and Religion,* 37-50, BAR British Series 212, Oxford

Bradley, J. 1991. Excavations at Moynagh Lough, Co. Meath. *Journal of the Royal Society of Antiquaries of Ireland* 111, 5-26

Bradley, R. 1990. *The Passage of Arms.* Cambridge University Press, Cambridge

Bradley, R. 1993. *Altering the Earth: the origin of monuments in Britain and Continental Europe,* Society of Antiquaries of Scotland, Edinburgh

Bibliography

Bradley, R. 1998. *The Significance of Monuments: on the shaping of human experience in Neolithic and Bronze Age Europe*, Routledge, London

Bradley, R. 2000. *An Archaeology of Natural Places*, Routledge, London

Bradley, R. 2002. *The Past in Prehistoric Societies*, Routledge, London/New York

Bradley, R., Entwistle, R. & Raymond, F. 1994. *Prehistoric Land Divisions on Salisbury Plain: the work of the Wessex Linear Ditches Project*, English Heritage, London

Brennand, M. & Taylor, M. 2003. The survey and excavation of a Bronze Age timber circle at Holme-next-the-sea, Norfolk, 1998-9. *Proceedings of the Prehistoric Society* 69, 1-84

Brinkkemper, O. 1991. *Wetland Farming in the Area to the South of the Meuse Estuary during the Iron Age and Roman Period: an environmental and palaeo-economic reconstruction.* Analecta 24, Leiden

Brück, J. 1999. Houses, life-cycles and deposition on Middle Bronze Age settlements in southern England. *Proceedings of the Prehistoric Society* 65, 145-66

Brück, J. (ed.) 2001. *Bronze Age Landscape: tradition and transformation*, Oxbow Books, Oxford

Bullied, A. & Gray, H. St G. 1911. *The Glastonbury Lake Village*, vol. 1. Privately published, Glastonbury

Cameron, C.M. & Tomka, S.A. (eds) 1993. *Abandonment of Settlements and Regions: ethnoarchaeological and archaeological approaches*, Cambridge University Press, Cambridge

Casparie, W.A. 1987. Bog trackways in the Netherlands. *Palaeohistoria* 29, 35-65

Champion, M. 2000. *Seahenge: a contemporary chronicle*, Barnwell's Timescape, Aylsham

Clark, J.G.D. 1954. *Excavations at Star Carr: an early Mesolithic site at Seamer near Scarborough, Yorkshire*, Cambridge University Press, Cambridge

Clark, J.G.D. 1972. *Star Carr: a case study in bioarchaeology*, Addison-Wesley, Massachusetts

Clarke, D.L. 1972. *Models in Archaeology.* Methuen, London

Coles, B.J. 1995. *Wetland Management: a survey for English Heritage*, English Heritage/WARP, London/Exeter

Coles, B.J. 1999. Somerset and the Sweet conundrum. In A.F. Harding (ed.) *Experiment and Design: archaeological studies in honour of John Coles*, 163-9, Oxbow Books, Oxford

Coles, B.J. 2004. Steps towards the heritage management of wetlands in Europe. *Journal of Wetland Archaeology* 4, 185-99

Bibliography

Coles, B.J. & Coles, J.M. 1986. *Sweet Track to Glastonbury*, Thames & Hudson, London

Coles, B.J. & Coles, J.M. 1989. *People of the Wetlands: bogs, bodies and lake-dwellers*, Thames & Hudson, London

Coles, B.J. & Coles, J.M. 1992. Passages of time. In *Archäologische Mitteilungen aus Nordwestdeutschland* 15, Oldenburg 1992, Seite 5-21

Coles, B.J. & Olivier, A. (eds) 2001. *The Heritage Management of Wetlands in Europe*, Europae Archaeologiae Concilium/WARP, Brussels/Exeter

Coles, J.M. 2001. Energetic activities of commoners. *Proceedings of the Prehistoric Society* 67, 19-48

Coles, J.M. & Coles, B.J. 1996. *Enlarging the Past: the contribution to wetland archaeology*, Society of Antiquaries of Scotland/WARP, Edinburgh/Exeter

Coles, J.M. & Hall, D. 1998. *Changing Landscapes: the ancient Fenland*, Cambridgeshire County Council/Wetland Archaeology Research Project, Cambridge

Coles, J.M. & Lawson, A.J. (eds) 1987. *European Wetlands in Prehistory*, Clarendon Press, Oxford

Coles, J.M. & Minnett, S. 1995. *Industrious and Fairly Civilized: the Glastonbury Lake Village*, Somerset County Council, Taunton

Conneller, C. & Schadla-Hall, T. 2003. Beyond Star Carr: the Vale of Pickering in the 10th millennium BC. *Proceedings of the Prehistoric Society* 69, 85-105

Cooney, G. 2000. *Landscapes of Neolithic Ireland*. Routledge, London

Cory, V. 1985. *Hatfield and Axholme: an historical review*. Providence Press, Ely

Cosgrove, D.E. & Daniels, S. (eds) 1988. *The Iconography of Landscape*, Cambridge University Press, Cambridge

Cosgrove, D.E. 1984. *Social Formation and Symbolic Landscape*, University of Wisconsin Press, Madison

Cosgrove, D.E. 1993. Landscapes and myths, gods and humans. In B. Bender (ed.) *Landscape: politics and perspectives*, Berg, Providence/Oxford, 281-305

Cox, M, Starker, V. & Taylor, D. (eds) 1995. *Wetlands: archaeology and nature conservation*, HMSO, London

Croes, D.R. 2001. Birth to death: Northwest Coast wet site basketry and cordage artefacts reflecting a person's life-cycle. In B.A. Purdy (ed.) *Enduring Records: the environmental and cultural heritage of wetland sites,* 92-109, Oxbow Books, Oxford

Croes, D.R. & Foster, R. 2004. Perishable artifacts from Northwest coast sites – a critical need for Native American expertise. In *Wetland Archaeology Research Project 10th International Confer-*

Bibliography

ence: Wet Sites Connections: April 1-5, 2004, Olympia, Washington, Conference Pre-prints, 2-7, Olympia

Crone, A. 1993. Crannogs and chronologies. *Proceedings of the Society of Antiquaries of Scotland* 123, 245-54

Crone, A. 2000. *The History of a Scottish Lowland Crannog: excavations at Buiston, Ayrshire 1989-90*, Scottish Trust for Archaeological Research, Edinburgh

Crone, A., Henderson, J.C. & Sands, R. 2001. Scottish crannogs: construction, collapse and conflation. Problems of interpretation. In B. Raftery & J. Hickey (eds) *Recent Developments in Wetland Research*, 55-64, Seandálaíocht: Dept. of Archaeology, University College, Dublin Monograph Series, vol. 2, Dublin

Cross, S., Murray, C., Ó Neill, J. & Stevens, P. 2001. Derryville Bog: a vernacular landscape in the Irish midlands. In B. Raftery & J. Hickey (eds) *Recent Developments in Wetland Research*, 87-98, Seandálaíocht: Dept. of Archaeology, University College, Dublin Monograph Series, vol. 2, Dublin

Crumlin-Pedersen, O. & Munch Thye, B. 1995. *The Ship as Symbol in Prehistoric and Medieval Scandinavia*, National Museum of Denmark, Copenhagen

Cunliffe, B. 1995. *Danebury: an Iron Age hillfort in Hampshire*, vol. 6. *A Hillfort Community in Perspective*, CBA Research Report 102, York

Cushing, F. 1897. Exploration of ancient Key-dweller remains on the Gulf Coast of Florida. *Proceedings of the American Philosophical Society* 25, 329-448

Davey, P.J. 1973. Bronze Age metalwork from Lincolnshire. *Archaeologia* 104, 51-127

Dinnin, M. & Van de Noort, R. 1999. Wetland habitats, their resource potential and exploitation. In B. Coles, J. Coles & M. Schou Jørgensen (eds) *Bog Bodies, Sacred Sites and Wetland Archaeology*, 69-78, WARP, Exeter

Edmonds, M. 1999. *Ancestral Geographies of the Neolithic: landscapes, monuments and memory*, Routledge, London

Egloff, M. 1987. 130 years of archaeological research in Lake Neuchatel, Switzerland. In J.M. Coles & A. Lawson (eds) *European Wetlands in Prehistory*, 23-32, Clarendon Press, Oxford

Egloff, M. 1988. Recent archaeological discoveries in Lake Neuchatel, Switzerland: from the palaeolithic to the Middle Ages. In B. Purdy (ed.) *Wet Site Archaeology*, 15-30, Telford Press, New Jersey

English Heritage 1991. *Exploring Our Past*, English Heritage, London

Evans, C. 1990. Review of B.A. Purdy (ed.) 1988. *Wet Site Archaeology* [Telford Press, New Jersey], *Proceedings of the Prehistoric Society* 56: 339-40

Evans, J.G. 1992. River valley bottoms and archaeology in the Holocene. In B. Coles (ed.) *The Wetland Revolution in Prehistory*, 47-53, The Prehistoric Society/WARP, London/Exeter

Field, N. & Parker Pearson, M. 2003. *Fiskerton. An Iron Age timber causeway with Iron Age and Roman votive offerings: the 1981 excavations*, Oxbow Books, Oxford

Fischer, A., Schlichtherle, H. & Pétrequin, P. 2004. Steps towards the heritage management of wetlands in Europe: response and reflection. *Journal of Wetland Archaeology* 4, 201-7

Foster, R. & Croes, D.R. 2002. Tribal-archaeological cooperative agreement. A holistic cultural resource management approach. *Journal of Wetland Archaeology* 2, 25-38

Frazer, W.O. & Tyrrell, A. (eds) 2000 *Social Identity in Early Medieval Britain*, Leicester University Press, London/New York

Fredengren, C. 2001. Poor people's crannogs. *Archaeology Ireland* 15, 24-5

Fredengren, C. 2002. *Crannogs: a study of people's interaction with lakes, with particular reference to Lough Gara in the north-west of Ireland*, Wordwell, Bray

Gearey, B.R. 2002. 'Foule and flabby quagmires': the archaeology of wetlands. *Antiquity* 76, 896-900

Geertz, C. 1983. *Local Knowledge: further essays in interpretive anthropology*, Basic Books, New York

Geertz, C. 2000. *Available Light: anthropological reflections on philosophical topics*, Princeton University Press, Princeton

Gerritsen, F. 1999. The cultural biography of Iron Age houses and the long-term transformation of settlement patterns in the southern Netherlands. In C. Fabech & J. Ringtved (eds) *Settlement and Landscape. Proceedings of a conference in Arhus, Denmark, May 4-7, 1998*, Hojbjerg, 139-48

Gerritsen, F. 2003. *Local Identities: landscape and community in the late prehistoric Meuse-Demer-Scheldt region*, Amsterdam University Press, Amsterdam

Giblett, R.J. 1996. *Postmodern Wetlands: culture, history, ecology*, Edinburgh University Press, Edinburgh

Giles, M. 2001. *Open-weave, Close-knit: archaeologies of identity in the later prehistoric landscape of East Yorkshire*, unpublished PhD thesis, University of Sheffield

Gosden, C. 1994. *Time and Social Being*, Routledge, London/New York

Gregory, C. 1980. Gifts to men and gifts to god: gift exchange and capital accumulation in contemporary Papua. *Man* 25, 628-52

Hafner, A. 2004. Underwater archaeology: lake-dwellings below the water surface. In Menotti, F. (ed.) 2004. *Living on the Lake in prehistoric Europe: 150 years of lake-dwelling research*. Routledge, London/New York

Bibliography

Hall, D. & Coles, J. 1994. *Fenland Survey : an essay in landscape and persistence*, English Heritage, London

Harding, A.F. 2000. *European Societies in the Bronze Age*, Cambridge University Press, Cambridge

Harris, M. 1998. The rhythm of life: seasonality and sociality in a riverine village. *Journal of the Royal Anthropological Institute* 4 (1), 65-82

Harris, M. 2000. *Life on the Amazon: the anthropology of a Brazilian peasant village* Oxford University Press, Oxford

Haselgrove, C., Armitt, I., Champion, C., Creighton, J., Gwilt, A., Hill, J.D., Hunter, F. & Woodward, A. 2001. *Understanding the British Iron Age: an agenda for action*, Wessex Archaeology, Salisbury

Hayes, P. 1988. Roman to Saxon in the south Lincolnshire fens. *Antiquity* 62, 321-6

Healey, F. 1996. *Fenland Project 11. Wissey Embayment. The Evidence for pre-Iron Age Occupation*. East Anglian Archaeology 78

Hencken, H. O'Neill. 1936. Ballinderry crannóg no. 1. *Proceedings of the Royal Irish Academy* 43 sect. C, no. 5, 103-239

Hencken, H. O'Neill. 1942. Ballinderry crannóg no. 2. *Proceedings of the Royal Irish Academy* 47 sect. C, no. 1, 1-76

Hencken, H. O'Neill 1950. Lagore crannóg: an Irish royal residence of the seventh to tenth century AD. *Proceedings of the Royal Irish Academy* 53 sect. C, no. 1, 1-248

Henderson, J.C. 1998. Islets through time: the definition, dating and distribution of Scottish crannogs. *Oxford Journal of Archaeology* 17 (2), 227-44

Hill, J.D. 1995. *Ritual and Rubbish in the Iron Age of Wessex*, BAR British Series 242, Oxford

Hirsch, E. & O'Hanlon, M. (eds) 1995. *The Anthropology of Landscape: perspectives on place and space*, Clarendon Press, Oxford

Hodder, I. 1999. *The Archaeological Process: an introduction*, Blackwell, London

Holley, M.W. 2000. *The Artificial Islets / Crannogs of the Central Inner Hebrides*. BAR British Series 303, Oxford

Ingold, T. 1993. The temporality of the landscape. *World Archaeology* 25 (2), 24-174

Ingold, T. 1995. Building, dwelling, living: how animals and people make themselves at home in the world. In M. Strathern (ed.) *Shifting Contexts: transformations in anthropological knowledge*, Routledge, London

Jacomet, S. 2004. Archaeobotany: a vital tool in the investigation of lake-dwellings. In F. Menotti (ed.) *Living on the Lake in Prehistoric Europe: 150 years of lake-dwelling research*, 162-77, Routledge, London/New York

157

Bibliography

James, S. 1999. *The Atlantic Celts: ancient people or modern invention?* British Museum Press, London

Johnson, M. 1999. *Archaeological Theory: an introduction.* Blackwell, London

Keane, M. 1995. Lough More, Co. Mayo: the crannog. In *Irish Archaeological Wetland Unit Transactions* 4, 167-82, University College Dublin, Dublin

Keller, F. 1866. *The Lake-Dwellings of Switzerland and Other Parts of Europe*, Longman Green, London

Kelly, F. 1997. *Early Irish Farming*, Dublin Institute of Advanced Studies, Dublin

Koch, E. 1999. Neolithic offerings from the wetlands of eastern Denmark. In B. Coles, J. Coles & M. Shou Jørgenson (eds) *Bog Bodies, Sacred Sites and Wetland Archaeology*, 125-32, WARP, Exeter

Kopytoff, I. 1986. The cultural biography of things: commoditization as process. In A. Appadurai (ed.) *The Social Life of Things: commodities in cultural perspective*, 64-91, Cambridge University Press, Cambridge

Lamb, C. 2003. The Eden project: can the arid lands of the Marsh Arabs ever be restored? in *Sunday Times Magazine*, 27 July 2003, 20-8

Larsson, L. 2001. South Scandinavian wetland sites and finds from the Mesolithic and the Neolithic. In B. Purdy (ed.) *Enduring Records: the environmental and cultural heritage of wetlands*, 158-71, Oxbow Books, Oxford

Legge, A.J. & Rowley-Conwy, P.A. 1988. *Star Carr Revisited: a reanalysis of the large mammals*, Birkbeck College, London

Lopez, B. 1986. *Arctic Dreams: imagination and desire in a northern landscape*, Harvill Press, New York

Louwe Kooijmans, L.P. 1993. Wetland exploitation and upland relations of prehistoric communities in the Netherlands'. In J. Gardiner (ed.) *Flatlands and Wetlands: current themes in East Anglian archaeology*, 71-116, East Anglian Archaeology 50

Lucas, A.T. 1989. *Cattle in Ancient Ireland*, Boethius Press, Kilkenny

Lucas, G. 2005. *The Archaeology of Time*, Routledge, London/New York

McDermott, C. 1998. The prehistory of the Offaly peatlands. In W. Nolan & T.P. O'Neill (eds.) *Offaly: History and Society*, 1-28, Geography Publications, Dublin

McErlean, T. & O'Sullivan, A. 2002. Foreshore tidal fishtraps. In T. McErlean, R. McConkey & W. Forsythe, *Strangford Lough: an archaeological survey of its maritime cultural landscape*, 144-80, Blackstaff Press, Belfast

McGrail, S. 2003. The sea and archaeology. *Historical Research* 76: 1-17

Bibliography

McOmish, D., Field, D. & Brown, G. 2002. *The Field Archaeology of the Salisbury Plain Training Area*, English Heritage, Swindon

Magny, M. 1993. Une nouvelle mise en perspective des sites archéologiques lacustres: les fluctuations holocènes des lacs jurassiens et subalpins. *Gallia-Préhistoires* 35, 253-82

Maxwell, G. 1957. *A Reed Shaken by the Wind*. Longmans, London

Meddens, F.M. 1996. Sites from the Thames Estuary wetlands, England, and their Bronze Age use. *Antiquity* 70, 325-34

Mellars, P.A. & Dark, P. 1998. *Star Carr in Context*, McDonald Institute Monograph, Cambridge

Menotti, F. 1999. The abandonment of the ZH-Mozartstrasse Early Bronze Age lake-settlement: GIS computer simulations of the lake-level fluctuation hypothesis. *Oxford Journal of Archaeology* 18(2), 143-55

Menotti, F. 2001. *The 'Missing Period': Middle Bronze Age lake-dwelling occupational hiatus in the northern Alpine region*. BAR International Series 968, Oxford

Menotti, F. 2003. Cultural response to environmental change in the Alpine lacustrine regions: the displacement model. *Oxford Journal of Archaeology* 22 (4), 375-96

Menotti, F. (ed.) 2004. *Living on the Lake in Prehistoric Europe: 150 years of lake-dwelling research*. Routledge, London/New York

Meskell, L. 2001. Archaeologies of identity. In Ian Hodder (ed.) *Archaeological Theory Today*, 187-213, Polity, Cambridge

Mitsch, W.J. & Gosselink, J.G. 1993. *Wetlands* (2nd edn), Van Nostrand Reinhold, New York

Moore, C., Murray, C., Stanley, M. & McDermott, C. 2003. Bogland surveys in Ireland: forty shades of brown. In J. Fenwick (ed.) *Lost and Found: discovering Ireland's past*, Wordwell, Dublin, 123-38

Moreland, J. 2001. *Archaeology and Text*, Duckworth, London

Morrison, I. 1985. *Landscape with Lake Dwellings: the crannogs of Scotland*, University Press, Edinburgh

Munro, R. 1882. *Ancient Scottish Lake-Dwellings or Crannogs*, David Douglas, Edinburgh

Murray, C. 2000. A wooden vessel from Co. Westmeath, Ireland, *NewsWARP*, 28, 7-8

Nicholson, E. & Clark, P. 2002. *The Iraqi Marshlands: a human and environmental study*, Politicos, London

O'Carroll, E. 2001. *The Archaeology of Lemonaghan – the story of an Irish bog*, Wordwell, Dublin

Ó Corráin, D. 1972. *Ireland before the Normans*, Gill and McMillan, Dublin

O'Neill, J. 2000. A summary of investigations by the Lisheen Archaeological Project. *Tipperary Historical Journal*, 173-90

Bibliography

O'Sullivan, A. 1998. *The Archaeology of Lake Settlement in Ireland*, Discovery Programme/Royal Irish Academy, Dublin

O'Sullivan, A. 2000. *Crannogs: lake-dwellings of early Ireland*, Town House, Dublin

O'Sullivan, A. 2001a. *Foragers, Farmers and Fishers in a Coastal Landscape: an intertidal archaeological survey of the Shannon Estuary*, Royal Irish Academy, Dublin

O'Sullivan, A. 2001b. Crannogs – places of resistance in the contested landscapes of early modern Ireland. In B. Bender & M. Winer (eds) *Contested Landscapes: landscapes of movement and exile*, 87-101, Berg, Oxford

O'Sullivan, A. 2001c. Crannogs in late medieval Gaelic Ireland, c. 1350 – c. 1600. In P.J. Duffy, D. Edwards & E. Fitzpatrick (eds) *Gaelic Ireland: land, lordship and settlement, c. 1250 – c. 1660*, 397-417, Four Courts Press, Dublin

O'Sullivan, A. 2003a. The Harvard Archaeological Expedition and the politics of the Irish Free State. *Archaeology Ireland* 66, 10-13

O'Sullivan, A. 2003b. A day in the life of a medieval fisherman ... and of intertidal archaeologists. In J. Fenwick (ed.) *Lost and Found: discovering Ireland's past*, 233-46, Wordwell, Dublin

O'Sullivan, A. 2003c. Place, memory and identity among estuarine fishing communities: interpreting the archaeology of early medieval fish weirs. *World Archaeology* 35, 449-68

O'Sullivan. A 2004. *The Social and Ideological Role of Crannogs in Early Medieval Ireland*, unpublished PhD thesis, National University of Ireland, Dublin

O'Sullivan, A. 2005. Medieval fishtraps on the Shannon estuary, Ireland: interpreting people, place and identity in estuarine landscapes. *Journal of Wetland Archaeology* 5, 65-77

Oelschlaeger, M. 1991. *The Idea of Wilderness: from prehistory to the age of ecology*, Yale University Press, New Haven/London

Olivier, A. & Van de Noort, R. 2002. *English Heritage Strategy for Wetlands*, English Heritage/University of Exeter, London/Exeter

Overing, J. & Passes, A. 2000. Conviviality and the opening up of Amazonian anthropology. In J. Overing & A. Passes (eds) *The Anthropology of Love and Anger: the aesthetics of conviviality in native Amazonia*, Routledge, London/New York

Parker Pearson, M. & Sydes, R.E. 1997. The Iron Age enclosures and prehistoric landscape at Sutton Common, S. Yorkshire. *Proceedings of the Prehistoric Society* 63, 221-59

Patterson, N. 1994. *Cattle Lords and Clansmen: the social structure of early Ireland*, University of Notre Dame Press, Notre Dame

Perini, R. 1988a (ed.). *Archeologia del legno*. Quaderni della Sezione Archeologica Museo Provinciale d'arte 4, Castello del Buoncon-siglio, Trento

Bibliography

Perini, R. 1988b (ed.). *Scavi archeologici nella zona palafiticola de Fiave-Carera* II, Trento

Pétrequin, P. 1989. *Les sites littoraux Néolithiques de Clairvaux-Les-Lacs (Jura). II Le Néolithique moyen*, Editions de la Maison des Sciences de l'homme, Paris

Pétrequin, P. 1997. *Les sites littoraux Néolithiques de Clairvaux-Les-Lacs et de Chalain (Jura). III Chalain station 3 3200-2900 av. J.-C.*, Editions de la Maison des Sciences de l'homme, Paris (2 vols)

Pétrequin, P. & Bailly, M. 2004. Lake-dwelling research in France: from climate to demography. In F. Menotti (ed.) *Living on the lake in Prehistoric Europe: 150 years of lake-dwelling research*, Routledge, London/New York, 36-49

Pierce Erikson, P. 2002. *Voices of a Thousand People: The Makah Cultural and Research Center*, University of Nebraska Press, Lincoln/London

Pryor, F. 1998. *Etton: excavations at a Neolithic causewayed enclosure near Maxey, Cambridgeshire, 1982-87*, English Heritage, London

Pryor, F. 2001. *The Flag Fen Basin: archaeology and environment of a fenland landscape*, English Heritage, Swindon

Purdy, B.A. (ed.) 2001. *Enduring Records: the environmental and cultural heritage of wetland sites*, Oxbow Books, Oxford

Raftery, B. 1990. *Trackways through Time: archaeological investigations on Irish bog roads, 1985-1989*. Headline, Rush

Raftery, B. 1996. *Trackway Excavations in the Mountdillon Bogs, Co. Longford, 1985-1991*, The Irish Archaeological Wetland Unit, Dublin

Rippon, S. 2000. *The Transformation of Coastal Wetlands: exploitation and management of marshland landscapes in North West Europe during the Roman and medieval periods*, Oxford University Press, Oxford

Ruoff, U. 2004. Lake-dwelling studies in Switzerland since 'Meilen 1854'. In F. Menotti (ed.) *Living on the Lake in Prehistoric Europe: 150 years of lake-dwelling research*, 9-21, Routledge, London/New York

Scarre, C. 1989. Review of J.M. Coles & A.J. Lawson (eds) 1987 *European Wetlands in Prehistory* [Clarendon Press, Oxford]. *Proceedings of the Prehistoric Society* 55, 274-5

Schama, S. 1996. *Landscape and Memory*, HarperCollins, London

Schibler, J. 2004 Bones as a key for reconstructing the environment, nutrition and economy of the lake-dwelling societies. In F. Menotti (ed.) *Living on the Lake in Prehistoric Europe: 150 years of lake-dwelling research*, 144-61, Routledge, London/New York

Schlichtherle, H. 1997. *Pfahlbauten rund die Alpen*, Theiss, Stuttgart

Schlichtherle, H. 2004. Lake-dwellings in south-western Germany: history of research and contemporary perspectives. In F. Menotti (ed.) *Living on the Lake in Prehistoric Europe: 150 years of lake-dwelling research*, 22-35, Routledge, London/New York

Bibliography

Shanks, M. & Tilley, C. 1987. *Social Theory and Archaeology*, Polity, Cambridge

Shennan, S. 2000. Population, culture history and the dynamics of culture change. *Current Anthropology* 41 (5), 811-35

Smith, B. 1985. *A Palaeoecological Study of Raised Mires in the Humberhead Levels*, unpublished PhD thesis, University of Wales

Smith, R. 2004. *A Marsh through Time: saving Sutton Common*, Halsgrove, Tiverton

Soffer, O., Adovasio, J.M. & Hyland, D.C. 2001. Perishable technologies and invisible people: nets, baskets and 'Venus' wear ca. 26,000 BP. In B. Purdy (ed.) *Enduring Records: the environmental and cultural heritage of wetlands*, 233-45, Oxbow Books, Oxford

Stanley, M. 2003. Archaeological survey of Irish bogs: information without understanding? *Journal of Wetland Archaeology* 3, 61-74

Stocker, D. & Everson, P. 2003. The straight and narrow way: Fenland causeways and the conversion of the landscape in the Witham valley, Lincolnshire. In M. Carver (ed.) *The Cross goes North: processes of conversion in Northern Europe AD 300-1300,* 271-88, Woodbridge Medieval Press, York

Stout, M. 1997. *The Irish Ringfort*, Four Courts Press, Dublin

Stovin Ms = The Stovin Manuscript, ed. C. Jackson, *Yorkshire Archaeological and Topographical Journal* B, 194-238

Therkorn, L., Brandt, R.W., Pals, J.P., Taylor, M. 1984. An early Iron Age farmstead: Site Q of the Assendelver Polders Project. *Proceedings of the Prehistoric Society* 50, 351-73

Thesiger, W. 1959. Marsh dwellers of Southern Iraq. *National Geographic Magazine*, Feb. 1959

Thesiger, W. 1964. *The Marsh Arabs*, Longman, Green and Co., London

Tilley, C. 1991. Review of B. & J. Coles (1989) *People of the Wetlands. Proceedings of the Prehistoric Society* 57, 214-15

Tilley, C. 1994. *A Phenomenology of Landscape: places, paths and monuments,*. Berg, London

Tilley, C. 1999. *Metaphor and Material Culture*, Blackwell, Oxford

Tilley, C. 2001. Thinking places. Review of R. Bradley (2000) *An Archaeology of Natural Places. Cambridge Journal of Archaeology* 11, 130-2

Tilley, C. 2004. *The Materiality of Stone: explorations in landscape phenomenology*, Berg, Oxford

Trigger, B. 1990. *A History of Archaeological Thought*, Cambridge University Press, Cambridge

Tringham, R. 1991. Households with faces: the challenge of gender in architectural remains. In J. Gero & M. Conkey (eds) *Engendering Archaeology: women and prehistory*, 93-131, Blackwell, Oxford

Tringham, R. 1995. Archaeological houses, households, housework

Bibliography

and the home. In D.N. Benjamin, D. Stea & D. Saile (eds) *The Home: words, interpretations, meanings and environments*, Avebury, Aldershot, 79-107

Van de Noort, R. 1995. 'West Furze: the reconstruction of a monumental wetland landscape'. In R. Van de Noort & S. Ellis (eds) *Wetland Heritage of Holderness, an Archaeological Survey*, 323-34, University of Hull, Hull

Van de Noort, R. 2004a. An ancient seascape: the social context of seafaring in the Early Bronze Age. *World Archaeology* 35, 404-15

Van de Noort, R. 2004b. *The Humber Wetlands: the archaeology of a dynamic landscape*, Windgather Press, Bollington

Van de Noort, R. & Ellis, S. (eds) 1999. *Wetland Heritage of the Vale of York, an Archaeological Survey*, University of Hull, Hull

Van de Noort, R., Middleton, R., Foxon, A., & Bayliss, A. 1999. The 'Kilnsea-boat', and some implications from the discovery of England's oldest plank boat. *Antiquity* 73, 131-5

Van de Noort, R. & Panter, I. 2001. Archaeology and Rubbish. *Past* 36: 2

Van der Sanden, W. 1996. *Through Nature to Eternity: the bog bodies of Northwest Europe*, Batavia Lion International, Amsterdam

Van der Sanden, W. 2001. From stone pavement to temple – ritual structures from wet contexts in the province of Drenthe, the Netherlands. In B. Purdy (ed.) *Enduring Records: the environmental and cultural heritage of wetlands*, 132-47, Oxbow Books, Oxford

Van Gennep, A. 1908. *Les Rites de Passage*, Emile Nourry, Paris

Warner, R.B. 1994. On crannógs and kings: (part 1). *Ulster Journal of Archaeology* 57, 61-9

Welch, A.A., Lund, E., Amiano, P., Dorronsoro, M., Brustad, M., Kumle, M., Rodriguez, M., Lasheras, C., Janzon, L., Jansson, J., Luben, R., Spencer, E.A., Overvad, K., Tjonneland, A., Clavel-Chapelon, F., Linseisen, J., Klipstein-Grobusch, K., Benetou, V., Zavitsanos, X., Tumino, R., Galasso, R., Bueno-De-Mesquita, H.B., Ocke, M.C., Charrondiere, U.R. & Slimani, N. 2002. Variability of fish consumption within the 10 European countries participating in the European Investigation into Cancer and Nutrition (EPIC) study. *Public Health Nutrition*, Dec. 5, 1273-85

Wells, P.S. 2001. *Beyond Celts, Germans and Scythians: archaeology and identity in Iron Age Europe*. Duckworth, London

Whiting, C.E. 1936. Excavations on Sutton Common, 1933, 1934 and 1935. *Yorkshire Archaeological Journal* 33, 57-80

Whittle, A. 1996. *Europe in the Neolithic*, Cambridge University Press, Cambridge

Wilkinson, T. & Murphy, P. 1995. *The Archaeology of the Essex Coast: The Hullbridge Survey*, EAA 52, Norwich

Wood-Martin, M.G., 1886. *The Lake-Dwellings of Ireland, Or, Ancient*

Bibliography

Lacustrine Habitations of Erin commonly called Crannogs, Hodges, Figgis and Co., Dublin

Wright, E.V. 1990. *The Ferriby Boats: seacraft of the Bronze Age*, Routledge, London

Wright, E.V., Hedges, R., Bayliss, A. & Van de Noort, R. 2001. New AMS dates for the Ferriby boats; a contribution to the origin of seafaring. *Antiquity* 75, 726-34

Young, G. 1976. Water dwellers in a desert world. *National Geographic Magazine* 149 (4), April 1976, 502-22

Young, G. 1977. *Return to the Marshes: life with the Marsh Arabs of Iraq*, Collins, London

Zvelebil, M. 2003. Enculturation of Mesolithic landscapes. In L. Karsson (ed.) *Mesolithic on the Move*, 65-73, Oxbow Books, Oxford

Index

This index includes site and place names, and principal researchers, projects and institutions mentioned in the text.

DATE DUE

DEC 0 2007	